CW01667337

12 BUSINESS LESSONS FROM RUNNING AN ULTRA MARATHON

The ultimate guide to setting, planning and delivering business and running goals way beyond your comfort zone.

Trevor Lee

Business Presentation Coach, Sales Energiser, Podcast Host, Business Speaker and now Ultra Runner

Trevor Lee Media Ltd

THE TECHNICAL BIT

Published by Trevor Lee Media Ltd

Cover design by Rebecca Morton of Redsnapper Design

Back cover photo by Figolux Ltd

For permission requests, please contact the publisher at:

Trevor Lee Media
℅ 13 Church Street
Helston
Cornwall
TR13 8TD
UK
trevor@trevorleemedia.co.uk

Every effort has been made to ensure all references are accurate - we apologise if that isn't the case and will amend in future editions.

To talk to Trevor about sharing business lessons from 44@60 as a keynote speaker at your business event, please contact Trevor via trevor@trevorleemedia.co.uk or on 07785 390717

ISBN: 978 -1 -7398737-0-7

ACKNOWLEDGEMENTS

When I announced I was going to run 44 miles to 'celebrate' turning 60, little did I realise that the 'bravado' (if that is what it was) of the moment would result in a fabulous journey, at the heart of which were numerous amazing people whose support, advice, generosity and encouragement were just unbelievable.

My sincere gratitude to everyone who helped make 'Running 44@60' possible:

Running advisors who came on the Running 44@60 podcast and shared tons of top tips.

Sponsors who, along with Masterclass hirers and participants, helped me smash my fundraising target.

My crew on the day, who provided invaluable motivational support as well as food, drink and lollipops.

Runners generally, who were a great source of encouragement, and had to tolerate me constantly talking about the 'Classic Quarter'

I've attempted to list you all in the appendix

Collectively you inspired me to take the lessons I learnt from the planning and executing of the run into the business world. There are numerous similarities.

I hope this book inspires you to set yourself a Big, Hairy, Audacious running challenge or a Big, Hairy, Audacious business challenge. Ideally both.

THE CLASSIC QUARTER COURSE

44 and a bit miles from the UK's most Southerly Point - Lizard Point - to the most Westerly - Lands End.

All along the South West Coastal Path

Event Date : May 22nd 2021

Start Time - 07:05

Finish Time - 20:05

Event Organiser: Endurancelife

HOW TO USE THIS BOOK

There are three parts to each section of this book:

The ideas, tips and advice I was given that enabled me to successfully complete the ultramarathon.

How to take those ideas, tips and advice and use them to start a business or get better and more successful in business.

Each business section has a checklist of top tips which any business, regardless of its age or development, can easily implement.

Interspersed are summaries of my training activities from when I announced I was taking on the challenge through to the event itself.

The training sections are designed to help you plan your training for an ultra run.

Overall, the book aims to inspire, enthuse and energise.

Whether you use it for business or running.

Or ideally both.

If you enjoy the book and it inspires you to set yourself a Big, Hairy, Audacious business or running Goal, get in touch and we can talk about you sharing your goal on one of my podcasts - for business 'Better Presentations More Sales', and for running 'Running 44@60'. Reach out to me on LinkedIn, or email me via podcast@trevorleemedia.co.uk.

CONTENTS:

1.
I'M NOT A RUNNER

My greatest running achievement as a youngster was 'winning' the egg 'n' spoon race at the local primary schools sports day. I say 'winning' because when they called out the first three to collect coloured ribbons, I wasn't called. There was no video replay and no appeal. I've still no idea what happened. Not that 50+ years later I'm still dwelling on it!

Like most kids, we ran without realising. We ran when playing football and cricket. We ran to and from each other. We ran to hide during hide and seek. I was quite handy at the bean bag race, but living in a rural village with a school of around 50 pupils, running was only really organised on sports day.

After a second go at acquiring two minimum A level grades I took up a place on the Human Movement Studies degree at Nonington College in September 1980. I was average at most sports, and athletics was one of the 'modules' but I was more interested in throwing a javelin than learning how to run. I often wonder what it would be like to go back and re-do that degree. My greatest sporting achievement at College was winning the egg throwing competition, at the Guinness games held at Surrey University in the summer of 1983.

I left college in 1983 and I don't really remember doing any specific running, with the exception of the Retford 10k circa 1987 (I was the sales manager of the Retford Times between 1986 and 1988), until around 1991 when working in Swansea for the South Wales Evening Post I have some notes which suggest that I did start to do some event running. In 1992 I did a series of 10k's (10 kilometre races) and according to those notes I was very consistent finishing all races in around 44 or 45 minutes with a best of 44:06 - which still is my PB - not sure there's any danger of that being broken .... but you never know!

My college friends Neil and Christine Anthony, who were very good runners, persuaded me in October 1992 to run with them in the Cardiff Half Marathon. This was quite a step up from the 10k's. Nevertheless, I did some training, although I have no record to show just how much and how long - I suspect not much, as I can't remember running anything like eight or ten miles. Those were the days before GPS and Strava, and although I had kept race details on a scrap of paper, no training runs were recorded.

'DIVING INTO A CORNER SHOP FOR SOME MARS BARS'

So on the day of the 1992 Cardiff Half I almost certainly arrived well underprepared and with no idea what it was going to be like to run 13.1 miles.

This was confirmed at around the ten mile marker. The course took a 90° left-hand turn with a marshal on patrol directing runners around the turn. I was starving hungry due to my poor race preparation and could feel my energy levels had plummeted to something not far above zero, if at all. Behind the marshal I spied a corner shop. A corner shop meant Mars Bars. In some strange, zipped pocket thing that attached to my wrist I had a couple of pound coins. It was the only thing I carried with that day. This was my chance to eat! I side stepped the marshal much to his bemusement, particularly as he tried desperately to keep me on the 'course'. I ran into the shop found the Mars bars shelf, grabbed a couple, jumped the queue handed over the money, said 'keep the change', apologised to the queue and re-joined the race.

I eventually finished in two hours four minutes. My first half marathon at the age of 31, so a PB! 27 years later in 2019 I was delighted when I returned to run the Cardiff Half for the second time, and beat that time by nine minutes - admittedly with no corner shop stops along the way.

In the 27 years in between, gels and electrolyte drinks, and all manner of other running nutrition had arrived onto the running scene, and my preparation for 2019 was in a vastly different league to what it had been back in 1992.

In 1992 I had done no proper preparation. In 2019 preparation was meticulous. I bang on a lot about preparation when I'm working with business clients or running workshops or delivering webinars, particularly when I'm talking about presentations or sales pitches. You simply cannot underestimate how important thorough preparation is. It genuinely can make a difference between success or failure.

On an episode of my business podcast - Better Presentations More Sales - former war correspondent Shawn Rhodes talks about replacing hope with certainty. On the battlefield, preparation has to be meticulous if you are going to achieve your goals, one of which will be survival. Business isn't of course that extreme, but the lessons around preparation are very relatable. More on preparation and planning elsewhere in the book.

After Cardiff I've got no records of any running for another 11 years, during which time I got married, had children, furthered my career etc... the usual things that stop many people running, or at least give them a good excuse for not running!

It was autumn 2003 when my current running journey really started. Two and a half years earlier, in April 2011, I had celebrated my 40th birthday, and used it as a reason for getting together a number of old friends from my Nonington College days, and their families. We had all, at varying times, been through those years of life's journey where commitments and geography often prevent meet ups. No Zoom in those days. The 40th birthday meet up was a great success and became the catalyst for a decision to replicate it twice a year - spring and autumn.

Over a few beers at the autumn meet up in 2003, we started asking ourselves what we wanted to achieve by the time we were 45. I was 42 and a half at the time and 'blurted out', with the usual dose of beer-led bravado, that I wanted to run a marathon. My friends from the Cardiff half, Christine and Neil, said they would find a suitable race for me and give me plenty of time to prepare. They also advised that I should do two things: one was to start a running diary to record all my runs in the build-up to the marathon, and the second was to subscribe to Runner's World magazine, so that every month I would get a shot of motivation when the magazine landed on the doormat.

They quickly came back with a plan to run the Amsterdam marathon in October 2005. I had 2 years to get ready to go from next to no running to running a marathon. At that time marathon running had started to become a big thing for runners at all levels, including those who aimed to complete the marathon in all sorts of weird and wonderful guises. Remember the guy in 2020 who ran the London marathon as Big Ben and then struggled to get under the finishing arch. I had no plans to run Amsterdam in fancy dress.

My first running diary entry was for a run on the coastal path at Porthallow on the Lizard in Cornwall. The diary mentions a Dalmatian dog called Charlie who was more interested in running with me than he was listening to his owner wanting him to return to him. I imagine Charlie made it back.

The running diary is an old A4 hardback notebook, and I'm still using it today although there aren't that many blank pages left in it now and I'm having to write a lot smaller! In those early days I'd take several lines for a single run, and leave gaps between runs.

As the pages start to run out, only special runs are now allocated more than a single line! I still subscribe to Runner's World magazine, and it continues to give my running the same motivational lift.

I followed a training plan for about 18 months and I was confident of running close to my four hour target time.

My only training buddy was Sunny, my very enthusiastic Springer spaniel. I remember going for 20 mile runs around the back roads where we lived near Coverack, and with Sunny off the lead I reckon she covered 25, maybe even more. We would get back and I'd had enough. She would be ready to go again a few minutes later!

Around 12 miles into the Amsterdam marathon I was bang on schedule for finishing in just under my target time of 4 hours. But then my left knee started to ache quite a lot. Post race someone suggested it might have been because the course was so flat and I'd be used to running up and down hills. Whatever the reason I slowed down and as the 9 minute mile pacemaker passed me it became clear that 4 hours was no longer realistic.

An early business lesson here. If the target becomes unrealistic, you have to re-adjust. There is no point in pursuing something you simply know realistically won't happen. So I readjusted and the target became 4:10 and then 4:15 and finally 4:20. In the end I think my official time was 4:20:19. I could have definitely been under 4:20 but the last 300 yards were in the 1928 Olympic stadium. It was such a great feeling running through the tunnel and waving to everyone in the stadium as though they were there just for me! They must have wondered who I thought I was!

I did another marathon in 2010 – the Eden Project Marathon in Cornwall. That was tough and I finished in around 4:52. I remember being determined not to walk up any of the numerous hills. That was a strategy I was to learn on the 44 miler definitely not to follow!

Apart from those two marathon years, my running diary shows that I was running on average around 35 times a year, so roughly once every 10 days - occasionally in an organised event but usually just with me and Sunny.

My running began to change when at the beginning of 2017 I discovered parkrun and started to go to National Trust-hosted parkruns most Saturdays - either at Lanhydrock near Bodmin, or Trelissick near Truro, where I was now living.

At Trelissick I bumped into a few people that I had originally met when I first came to Cornwall in 1993, and got involved in something called 'Hash Running'. It was a very sociable running experience - I think it was, and might still be, described as an activity 'for drinkers who have a running problem'.

Those Hash running friends persuaded me to join my local running club (Truro) which I eventually did in the autumn of 2018.

Even now I don't regard myself as a proper 'Runner' even though as I write this I have somehow become the 'Acting Chair' of Truro Running Club, I'm quite involved with the Trelissick parkrun, and seven months into my 61st year I've run three marathon + distance events compared with just two in my first 60 years.

I have really enjoyed my running experience. You can too, and you don't need to be the fastest or longest runner to do so. Just getting out there for a run from your front door, a parkrun, a club run or an organised event, will be uplifting regardless of how hard it is. And the beauty of running is you don't have to rely on being selected for a team, need to train constantly or invest in expensive kit.

We're all runners.

Like me you may end up being an accidental or circumstantial runner.

If I ever need motivating to 'get out the door' and go running I simply think of all the people, particularly those who are my age, who for whatever reason aren't able to run.

If you can walk you can potentially walk/run and then run.

It is so easy in life to give things up because you think you are 'too old' or you 'haven't got time' or you think you're 'no longer any good'.

Don't let those reasons stop you.

If you're reading this and you're not a runner but you would like to be check where your nearest parkrun is, register for free, print out your barcode and turn up in Saturday at 8.45am.

I'M NOT A BUSINESS PERSON

I described myself as an accidental runner and I suspect in business many people would regard themselves as accidental business people.

We tend to think of business people as those that are running large corporations, constantly making key decisions, driving a flashy car, looking for the next big deal to be done etc.

But of course there are literally hundreds of thousands of people, certainly here in the UK, who are running their own business.

If you are reading this book and have aspirations to be an ultra runner, as well as maybe having an aspiration to run your own business, then hopefully the content will be really useful to you, because without doubt the principles of planning, preparing and then running an ultramarathon are not dissimilar to planning and preparing to launch and then run a business.

So what makes someone suddenly decide to become a business person, in the same way I decided I was going to become an ultra runner?

Circumstance undoubtedly plays a part. Many people start businesses because of an unexpected opportunity, which at the time may not have felt like an opportunity, particularly if they've been working for someone else and that job has, for whatever reason, come to an end and they now need to do something different.

That certainly happened to many people when COVID struck in early 2020. Jobs were furloughed or disappeared. Lots of people found themselves wondering what they were going to do. For some the answer became to start a business. You may be one of those.

And no doubt you had that moment when you started to think 'should I be launching a business?'

And then imposter syndrome kicks in. You start over-analysing your capabilities and experience. You think 'wow I've got no business experience, I'm not a business person, this is a ridiculous idea!'

If you have an ambition to run your own business, then don't let your inexperience or your lack of knowledge put you off. As I did when it came to ultra running, you can gain that knowledge, and you can – through the running equivalent of training – build that experience, if of course you have the hunger and desire to learn.

'LEARN, LISTEN, QUESTION, OBSERVE AND YOU CAN BE A BUSINESS PERSON'

I'm told a lot of start-up businesses fail because those that started them simply don't see the need to learn.

Through a third party programme, I have worked with a lot of new businesses over recent years, and most of them have been set up and are being run by people who would not think of themselves primarily as a business person.

They see themselves as an artist, a web designer, a gardener, a lifestyle coach, a bookkeeper etc... They are doing what they are good at, with the challenge being to take what they're good at and turn it into a business that is sustainable, in terms of generating sufficient income to enable them to keep running it.

And there's the link to my running adventure: I didn't know anything about ultra running in the same way that the new business start-up may not know anything about running a business, but if we take advantage of all the resources that are available to us, then in business terms we will be business people, even if we feel we are accidental business people.

I knew that the only way I was going to be successful, and success was measured in achieving the completion of the run, was by having to need to learn from running experts. And to me the same applies if you are starting a business. Learn from business experts as they will be a great source of advice, knowledge, tips, experience etc. and usually they are all very keen to share with beginners their knowledge and experience.

So very much like preparing and planning to run an ultramarathon you need to prepare and plan to run a successful business.

As you work your way through this book, you will see sections on specific things that you can adapt to a business context, and I hope that you will pick them up if you are thinking about or have recently started a business. I'm sure the many tips and ideas will be hugely beneficial to you as your business journey develops.

And of course there will be setbacks. Times when your business feels like it's floundering. It will be easy to think about giving up, especially if a good-looking job offer comes along. That's a point where you will need to make a decision: do I carry on, or take a job with someone else?

Circumstances may help decide your decision. But if you face a clear choice, then be realistic but with a touch of adventure thrown in. You've started this business, so what's stopping you continuing it? It might be early days and it might not be producing tons of money but if you believe in what you are doing and you believe in yourself, then you increase your chances of success.

I remember the first three months of my business back in 2012. I left my 29-year career on a Friday in mid-September and Trevor Lee Media (my Twitter name at the time) started on the following Monday. That Monday I was bought lunch by Kevin McCormick, a business consultant whom I had met when he did some work for the media company I worked for.

Kevin spent lunch offering valuable advice. As he went to pay, I checked my emails. There weren't any! Not one! It was a brand-new email account but nevertheless I was expecting at least a couple of 'buy this' emails!

Fortunately, emails did start to appear and, in the run up to Christmas, I did several pieces of work, and the numbers looked good. I'd had work from my former employer, a couple of friends etc... I was feeling good, despite having the worst ever answer to that immortal networking question 'what do you do?'

I joke about it now when I deliver networking masterclasses, but at the time my answer to that question was: 'I used to be the Managing Director of Cornwall and Devon Media and now I do lots of things.'

You can imagine the calvary charge that caused. Goodness knows what I expected but if I thought it was clients galore fighting over each other to get my door, I was very wrong!

However, the work I had picked up was making me feel good about things. Reality, though, was just around the corner.

Christmas 2012 came and went and 2013 started. I had nothing in the pipeline. My turnover for the next four months was a grand total of £180. That's £45 per month or about £10 a week. Now I was fortunate that I had resources to keep going. I also had lucrative job offers. I turned them down.

Then the breakthrough moment. On May 1st a business bought into one of my regular services for a year. It wasn't huge - I think the fee was £195 a month - but it was transformational in terms of confidence to keep going.

I was told, as I detail later, that during the ultra run, there would be times when I would suffer extreme doubt about my ability to keep going.

You will certainly experience that in your business, especially if it's a new one. It will be easy to give up, to think you're not cut out for this that you're not a 'business person'. But here's the thing. Virtually everyone, I'm told, has those same thoughts, same doubts. Read the biographies of those that run the biggest corporations and you'll find that self-doubt appears somewhere in their story.

Like them, you have two options: Crack on and give it your best shot, or give up. The same applies to an ultramarathon. There were numerous times when I could have thought 'this is a ridiculous idea'.

If you give up you'll never know what might have happened – so recognise that doubts will arise, sales will appear to be going nowhere, you'll think you're being a busy fool etc...

But don't give up.

SECTION SUMMARY - TOP BUSINESS TIPS: BECOME A BUSINESS PERSON

- What are you good at?

- Who could benefit from your experience and knowledge?

- Who has ‘pain’ points you could resolve?

- And from those jottings/ notes create a simple business plan - include the answers to these questions:
  1. What is your offer?
  2. Who is it aimed at?
  3. Why will they need it?
  4. How will they know about it?
  5. How will they buy it?

- Be prepared to learn

- Make connections

- Stay on top of your finances

- Don’t give up

- Work Hard

- Learn Hard

- You’re not an imposter. You can be a successful business person

RUNNING DIARY; 1ST HALF 2019

In 2018 I did 58 runs, many of which were parkruns, and in October I joined Truro Running Club - my first time as a member of a running club. Good timing as it turned out, given what I was to announce a few months later.

My running in 2019 started with two parkruns on January 1st – both new events for me - Penrose near Helston and Heartlands near Redruth. As several parkruns across the UK did that day, one started at 9am and one at 10.30am so people like me and my buddy Mark Trebilcock, could run both. Heartlands was a touch chaotic as they hadn't anticipated how many people would turn up, and they had decided that day to reverse the course, which was three full laps, a half lap and a quarter lap. Nevertheless, as with all parkruns, it is the taking part that counts, and doing 2 on the same morning was great.

The first 'race' of significance for me in 2019 was on February 23rd – the Looe 10, described in the promos as hillish and hellish – it certainly was! My time was just under 1:45 and it was comfortably my longest race for quite a long time. I must have been inspired by the Looe 10 because it was four days later on Wednesday the 27th of February at a conference, when I made my decision to do the 44 miler. Interestingly, I made no mention of it in my running diary. The entry for Feb 27th just confirms that I went as usual to the Wednesday running club meet and did around five miles.

Announcing my plan to run the Endurancelife Classic Quarter obviously encouraged me to do a bit more running and through the first four months of 2019, I averaged around 10 runs of varying sorts per month.

Parkruns and club night runs were added to with organised events as I was now able to represent Truro Running Club. In Cornwall there are two 'series' of running events each year. The Cornwall Grand Prix series runs through the calendar year. By the end of the year I 'qualified' for my first ever running trophy – a recognition that I had completed eight of the events. There are various tables produced after each Grand Prix event, and I did keep tabs on how I was doing in the 55-59 category. My aim was to be in the category top 10 for each event.

On April 22nd I actually won a race! Ok it was the Coverack 'fun run', but a win's a win! The run traditionally took place on Bank Holiday Monday. It is the kind of event you expect to see featured on a TV documentary about life in rural England. I'd taken part a few times. The average field for the 4.5 mile route was around 15 and I would normally finish around sixth or seventh.

2019 was different, and everything worked in my favour! Firstly, Easter was quite late into April. Secondly, the day after Easter Monday was the first day back for schools across the UK. That meant most of the fast tourists had gone home.

The field was reduced to just six. As we attached our homemade cloth numbers, a throw-back in itself to different times, I was eyeing up what was obviously going to be a small field.

Eventually the start line consisted of myself, an 11-year-old girl and her dad who had a dog with him, the owner of a local hotel, a young lad, and a lady called Lucy from the Newquay Road Runners who had completed the London Marathon the week before. If I finished, I was guaranteed a top six finish. A podium seemed on the cards.

The youngsters looked fit, but would they last the distance? The hotel owner didn't look that fit, and the lady from Newquay was probably still recovering from the London marathon. The big danger looked like the man with the dog. The youngsters, as you might expect, set off at quite a good lick, and I found myself in fourth or fifth position but after about a mile and a half or so I had caught them all up and I was actually in the lead.

For the vast majority of runners, leading a race is an unusual experience. It certainly was for me!

I hadn't expected to be in the lead, so I decided to press on. At just over three miles, we turned right off the back road onto a vehicle track which took us past a house that we had built a few years earlier.

I knew that the track was downhill but quite rocky. By this stage I had a reasonable lead, so I decided to leg it as fast as I could down this track, which went all the way down to Coverack, and then if I was still in the lead, hang on for the last half mile to the finish.

Having run that downhill track many times, I felt like I knew every inch of it so I pushed the go button and ran as fast as I could.

On the front at Coverack, there is a café which at the time was called the Harbour Lights. Commanding front seats in the café were my daughter, her grandmother and her cousin.

I'd told them pre-race that I would probably be about fifth or sixth coming through, and it would be great to get a photo or two.

They weren't therefore expecting me to emerge in the lead. Fortunately, my daughter's cousin Jenny spotted the fact that I was in the lead, so they did manage to get a photo. I've got my arm up signalling number one with my finger! It's the photo I use on my Facebook profile.

By now there is less than half a mile to go – past the cafe then uphill past the church, along the sea front before heading down some steps behind the old post office, back up some steps and a final 100 yards to the finish line near the pub, the Paris Hotel.

I avoided the temptation to look back until I was near to the steps. I looked back. There was no one in sight. I was going to win! If you're ever in such a position you need to make the most of the moment. I certainly did. I did several 360 degree 'doughnut' turns as I approached the tape, relishing what was happening. There was a decent crowd at the finish.

Indeed, in most races I always relish the final moments. I mentioned earlier about waving to the crowd when finishing the Amsterdam marathon.

It's the same in business. Enjoy your moments of success. When I first started some years ago running business 'masterclasses', every time someone booked a £45 place I did a jig around my office space!

In terms of timing, I was actually 2.5 minutes quicker than when I had run in it 2016 and only a couple of minutes down on my course PB from 2011. I jokingly suggested they should have an honours board in the snooker room, which doubles up as a changing room, listing all the winners. As I write I am still the defending champion, as the event didn't happen in 2020 or 2021 because of the pandemic.

At the beginning of May, I drove up to Lincolnshire to visit my Mum. I did the Market Rasen parkrun and then on the Sunday I did the North Lincs Half Marathon which was based in the Scunthorpe area. It was all on road with about 1,600 runners.

My target was 2:05, knowing that if I did get close to two hours I would be delighted.

I started off relatively quickly, with the first four miles in an average pace of around 8:30. The race had pacers so after the fast start, my aim was to try and avoid being overtaken by the nine minute pacer until as far into the race as possible. That would give me a chance of being close to two hours, maybe even under it.

I got to 10 miles in 1:27:38. I am pretty good at mental maths so, as in any race, I'm always doing calculations in my head. I was aware with 3.1 miles to go that ten minute mile pace to the end would get me under two hours. That was hugely motivating as I did think my days of running sub-two-hour half marathons had long gone.

I did 9:11 for mile 11 and 9:30 for mile 12, so I knew I was well inside a sub-two-hour.

I finished in 1:56:15, which turned out to be my fifth fastest half marathon ever – my PB is 1:43 something. It was a long drive back to Cornwall but my running had received a real lift and I got a shout out at the next Running Club club night.

Two weeks later, I ran what is called the Imerys Half. A tough course near St Austell, where I learnt a big lesson about hills in races!

There was one very big hill at around mile five. Everyone was walking up it. Not me though. I decided that walking up hills wasn't for me. I would run up even if it felt like I was going at the same pace as the walkers.

By the time I got to the top I was exhausted. It took me another five miles to recover, as other runners piled past me!

I eventually struggled in in 2:16, although I note from the running diary that I was very pleased to have run two half marathons in two weeks. That was almost certainly a first. It was also my third half marathon of the year.

At that point I'd only every run three half marathons in the same year once before, and it was only May so plenty of time to better that.

The hill experience was a lesson I would learn more about. My expert advisors who would emerge as the 44 miler got closer suggested that I run up hills in training but not in the race. I would also learn to use poles on the uphills.

The first time I walked up the notorious hill at the Trelissick parkrun, I landed a course PB.

This book is all about sharing learning experiences or lessons as I've called them. Tackling hills is very much one of those lessons.

2.

BIG, HAIRY, AUDACIOUS GOAL - BHAG

In February 2019 I was invited/hired to be session speaker at a business conference in Cornwall. The headline speaker was a guy called Jim Lawless. Jim had a concept called Taming Tigers – indeed he had a book by the same name – which in itself was one of the early business lessons of this adventure. If you want to get hired as a headline or keynote speaker, write a book.

I suspect the number of copies that you sell is pretty much irrelevant, it is just the fact that you have got a book and you can send a copy of the book to the organiser. They will probably never read it, but they assume because you've got a book you must be a top person / star speaker.

So, no guessing as to why I've written this book! No doubt by the time you're reading this, I'm headlining business gigs around the globe, getting paid zillions, appearing on chat shows and having an entourage the size of a premier league footballer.

And all because you bought this book! I owe you big time!

One of the learnings from Jim was that he had a formula: He had the book. He turned the book into a 90-minute business gig. He included the occasional video clip and news cutting from his story that added to his credibility.

And you should do the same. Build your story. Gather up the evidence that supports it - reviews, testimonials, press cuttings etc....

Back to Jim.

So, I'm listening to Jim talking about Taming Tigers - essentially a concept of setting yourself challenges and goals that are well outside your comfort zone.

Jim told two very good stories - another top tip: in business there will be times when you need to be a good storyteller - I don't mean spinning yarns or fairy-tales, I mean being able to articulate your idea or proposition in a way that makes it compelling and irresistible to whoever needs convincing, be they a bank manager, an investor, or a potential customer or supplier.

Telling a story will make your audience feel more receptive to you than if you are just banging out a series of slides with no real feeling or passion behind them.

I digress but I wanted to share the benefits of storytelling with you.

So back to Jim's story.

Firstly, he shared how he had set himself the bold goal of becoming the UK men's free dive record holder. To do that he needed a plan and lots of preparation. Themes that will keep reoccurring throughout this book. The plan worked. He achieved the record diving 101 metres in August 2010. The previous record was 77 metres. As of October 2021 the record is 120 metres set by Harry Chamas in September 2017.

Secondly, according to his story, Jim was speaking at an event when someone in the audience challenged him to use his theories on himself, and the upshot was that he was given 12 months to learn how to ride a racehorse to a standard where he would take part in a televised professional horserace. Jim had never sat on a horse before. He accepted a £1 bet, and we watched the televised recording of the moment when he achieved the goal.

The more I listened to Jim, the more I decided that running a third marathon to celebrate my landmark birthday in 2021 wasn't a big enough challenge. I still have the notes from listening to him where I have written down 'Classic Quarter' – which I knew very little about except that it took place on the coastal path in Cornwall and started not too far from where I had spent many years living as the family grew up.

Over lunchtime I googled Classic Quarter to discover that it was a run on the coastal path from the UK's most southerly point, Lizard Point, to the most westerly point Land's End. Effectively you are running a quarter of the compass, hence the name 'Classic Quarter'. It immediately felt like an iconic event. I also discovered it was 44 miles, which was only 37 miles more than the distance that, at the time, I thought was a long way!

'OUT OF NOWHERE I'M ANNOUNCING I'M GOING TO RUN 44 MILES'

My speaking session was in the afternoon and, along with two or three others, I was invited to introduce myself to the audience, which was probably 130-150 people, and asked what I had learnt in the morning.

I happened to be sitting next to Jim – although I confess that having decided what I was going to announce, I made sure that I did get to sit next to him.

There's another business tip for you. Make things that appear lucky or accidental happen. I ensured I positioned myself as we walked onto the platform in such a place that I would sit next to Jim. That wasn't luck. It was planned! You can do the same. Next time you go to a business conference or networking event that involves randomly sitting next to people, remove the randomness bit by identifying who you want to sit with. It might mean following them to a table or row of chairs, but everyone will be following just like you. The difference being that you are deliberately following someone, whilst most other people are going with the flow.

And then guess what? You find yourself sitting next to someone you have targeted as a potential customer. A conversation starts and you create interest, maybe even a follow up meeting. As is often the case, you can make your own luck!

Jim was sitting on the far side of the platform. I also knew that sitting next to him I would be the last of the afternoon speakers to be introduced – there's another top tip for you in business terms – whilst I would always suggest if you are presenting go first, but if you are being introduced consider trying to go last.

Being the last person to be introduced gave me the opportunity to have the biggest impact – and that's certainly what happened to me because all the others said fairly predictable things - 'I enjoyed Jim's talk', 'I thought Jim was great', 'I like Jim's point about...' and then I announced I was going to run 44 miles in two years' time!

It certainly created a big impact amongst the audience and resulted in a photo moment where I am shaking hands with Jim Lawless, accepting his £1 bet. (I let Jim off the £1 when he made a generous donation to my fundraising - thanks Jim!)

Without really realising it at that particular moment I had announced my Big, Hairy, Audacious Goal, or BHAG for short.

The term BHAG was familiar to me from my regional media days. Towards the end of the 1990s, regional media was on a massive upward curve, and I remember my colleagues and I coming up with some ambitious plans to grow our various newspapers, and that's when we got introduced to the Big, Hairy, Audacious Goal – it is both exciting and scary all at once but it certainly gets the adrenaline flowing.

The BHAG is a goal that definitely takes you way out of your 'comfort zone', but which at the same time isn't unachievable, providing you commit to investing time and effort.

I vaguely remember leaving that event thinking about what I had announced I was going to do. Of course, one of the things about setting a very forward looking BHAG – in this case I knew that the event was at the beginning of June 2021 - was that if I needed them, I was going to get bags of opportunities to quietly drop the crazy idea I had launched.

And that's why section three is called 'Is this really happening?' Very much the equivalent of waking up the next morning and thinking 'did I really agree to do that?'

I did.

And so should you.

YOUR BUSINESS BHAG

Have you got a business BHAG?

Have you thought about having one?

Chances are you have business targets and plans. Often ones that you know are within reach of you achieving. In a sense we all play it safe when setting business targets.

Why? Essentially because we don't want to not hit the target. We don't want to be seen to fail, by our colleagues, our team, ourselves.

I've been there. In my media days we had to present a business plan to our head office team on an annual basis. That clearly included revenue and profit targets.

Ultimately it was a bit of a game. Our challenge was to set ourselves a goal that we thought was achievable and that our bosses thought was realistic, as well as worth dishing out a bonus for if it was achieved.

Then one year we were introduced to the BHAG. I can't recall exactly when and by whom, but I do recall the management team of which I was part of deciding to go for it.

We put together an ambitious, audacious plan. We would raise some of our prices by 15% instead of the usual 2.2%. We would give ad space away to private vendors to sell their household goods for free with no limit on the value of their items. We would significantly increase the size of our papers and raise our cover price by a whole 10p rather than the usual 1p.

You can imagine the reaction of the London team. They thought we had gone crazy. They were used to teams across the country 'selling' them plans that were overall cautious and game managed. Growth was set at a level the centres, as they were known, thought they could 'get away with'

Our plan was unheard of. Goodness knows what other centres thought when they were no doubt asked at their business plan meeting - 'the team in Cornwall are increasing their job advertising rate by 15%, why is yours going up 1.8%?'

So here's the thing. A BHAG sets a new level. A much higher level. It goes way beyond anything you have considered before. This is reach for the sky stuff.

But what happens if the BHAG isn't achieved? Is that a failure?

In theory you could say it is. Let's say your BHAG is to grow your customer base by 30% when traditionally in a good year it has grown by 5%.

If you are a relatively new company, a 30% growth in customers numbers may not be that much of an achievement. But if you are an established company 30% could be massive. 'Game changing', as they say.

'IT WILL BE EXCITING, SCARY, FUN, CHALLENGING AND GAME CHANGING'

So how do you know when your challenge moves from being a bigger than usual ambition target to a real life BHAG?

It's when you it scares you!
It's when your team thinks you're crazy to suggest it!
It's when the doubt side of you says 'that will never happen'.
And the excitement side of you says 'but just think what it would be like if we pulled it off'.

And actually that is a key thing to deal with if you're going to make this BHAG work. Before you overcome everyone else's doubts your need to overcome your own.

You have to convince yourself this could be achieved.

Then you need to 'sell it' to your colleagues, partners, team etc...
But don't sell them the numbers.
Sell them the vision.
The excitement.
The fun.
The scariness.

You should find that having a business BHAG will be all of those things.

It will generate focus, interest and, of course, a challenge.

Could you really do this?

Why not?

Sometimes when you are chasing modest business targets - let's say a 3-5% growth in a steady market - it just happens. A couple of big customers increase their spend, a new line does well, fewer customers move elsewhere. It doesn't take much to hit that target.

And how do you feel when that happens?

It looks good on the bottom line. But did it give you a big shot of adrenaline? Did you think - 'Wow I can't believe we've done that!'

I doubt it.

So imagine what it will feel like when you achieve your BHAG.

It will be like nothing that has gone before. Not just for you but for your team, your investors, etc...

Sounding good? Then set that BHAG!

In the section summary, I'll share how to do that.

But remember, this is not lip service. It's easy to say 'hey we're going to do this' and then get bogged down in the usual day to day stuff that means you 'forget' about the BHAG and it never happens.

I've worked with a number of businesses and individuals who are good at saying they're going to do stuff but then they never do.

That 'stuff' has included launching a new website, moving into a new area, expanding a service, speaking at events, starting a podcast, even writing a book.

And when I catch up with them a few weeks or months later and check in on progress guess what – nothing's happened. And then the excuses roll out - 'we've been really busy', 'a couple of people left', 'my dog ate my plan...'

Like with my run, it's easy to set the BHAG, and it's easy to left it drift and make excuses for it not happening.

Don't let that happen to you.

SECTION SUMMARY - TOP BUSINESS TIPS: SETTING A BHAG

- Look at your current business activities / goals
- Pick one that you feel passionate about doing significantly better
- One that if achieved would make you feel you've had a dose of the 'Wow' factor
- Start to imagine what it would be like to achieve this goal and the impact it would have on your business, your colleagues, your customers, your stakeholders
- Set the goal and the timescale to deliver it in
- Talk to people about it
- But be prepared for the 'are you crazy?' response
- When that happens, you know you're onto something
- Refer to it as your 'BHAG' (Big, Hairy, Audacious Goal)
- Don't let others convince you to 'water it down'
- Focus on it, plan for success, drive it forward

RUNNING DIARY; 2ND HALF 2019

I continued to take part in what is known as The Cornwall Grand Prix series, representing the club in lots of events usually between four and seven miles.

Most of these events are very traditional and have been taking place for many years.

I did another half marathon on August 4th at Indian Queens. My favourite race of 2019 was the Roseland August Trail or RAT organised by the excellent MudCrew. I did the 11 mile version.

It was, at around two and half hours, the longest run time-wise I had done since the Eden marathon in 2010.

The RAT festival has something for everyone, from the White Rat at 11 miles to the 'Bring Out Your Dead' - 24 hours of running a five mile loop with a maximum of 15 minutes allowed for rest at any one time. Check it out.

We were taken to the 11 mile start by coach. The same applies for the 20 mile (Red) and 32 (Black) versions. The routes all merge into one so everyone finishes at the event village. Different start times aim to avoid congestion on the course and aim to have everyone back for an evening of celebration.

This was first experience of a coastal path trail event and thus the first idea of running the same terrain I would experience in the Classic Quarter.

Coastal path runs are very different to road runs. Apart from different shoes, you have to think differently re timings. Road times are simply not comparable. I'm not sure if someone has devised a comparison chart which gives you some clues re timings. Something that says if your average mile time over 10 miles on the road is x you can expect it to be y when you run the coastal path. An opportunity for someone to create one?

As an example, it took 20 minutes to run the first mile of the White Rat. After the start, the route narrows and then encounters a couple of stiles, which inevitably means queueing, not just behind other White Ratters but to let any Red or Black Ratters through.

I ran the White Rat to have a fun time, enjoying banter with fellow runners and the crowds whilst also recording snippets for an episode of the Running 44@60 podcast and shooting a few video clips.

At the end of August, I did my first Classic Quarter route recce. I was helping organise at Mullion Cricket Club (fun fact - Mullion is the UK's most southerly cricket club) a six aside event. I took the opportunity of getting there early and running around about five and a half miles out and back along the coastal path towards Loe Bar beach near Helston.

Top tip: If you run the coastal path around Mullion treat yourself to refreshments afterwards (or during) at the lovely Porthmellin cafe. It has been in the same family for three generations. It is in Mullion Cove alongside the harbour and the Classic Quarter goes right past it. The delicious cakes are a just reward for your running efforts.

I finished with a lap around the cricket field, thinking yet again that running for two and a half hours was something monumental!

In September I set a parkrun PB of 24:29 at the Market Rasen Racecourse and then the following day I ran the 'Wolds Tough 10' in 1:36. Big thanks to the lovely people at Caistor Running Club for making me feel so welcome, including being part of your team photo! Mind you going from Cornwall where every run regardless of length involves numerous hills I'm convinced the 'Tough' bit might need a small t! For those who want a comparison, come to Cornwall in February and take part in the Looe 10 - described as 'hillish and hellish'!

Next up, the Cardiff half marathon 27 years after it was my first ever half marathon in 1992. Back in 1992 it had taken me another 12 years before I ran a second half marathon.

Could I beat my 1992 time of 2:04:05? Oh yes. 1:55:03. I was almost twice as old as I was on my first attempt, and I took nine minutes off my time. I was pleased with that!

A week later another first: back-to-back weekend half marathons. This one at the famous Eden Project. A very different course to Cardiff. I was around 2:11 but the key was proving that I could do the successive half marathons. The forerunner for 2021 back-to-back runs of this length where the back-to-back gap reduced from a week to a day.

In almost all of this, parkruns, club nights and other smaller distance races were all helping me get those valuable miles in the legs.

Half marathon number seven for 2019 was at Bedgebury Park in Kent, part of a weekend which involved a meet up with old friends and a parkrun at the same venue on the Saturday.

I went from Kent to Lincolnshire to spend a few days with my Mum. Just a few weeks later, on Christmas Eve she collapsed and died, completely out of the blue, whilst out with my brother. She was 83, took no medication and rarely visited her GP. We all expected her to break the family record for longevity held by her grandmother 'Nanny England' who outlived her daughter (my grandmother) in making it to 96.

As Mum had died suddenly and unexpectedly, an autopsy was needed. It revealed she had a bicuspid valve in her heart. She was born a valve short and would have never known this. Eventually two valves doing the work of three simply caught up with her.

Once this became known in early 2020, my brothers and I were advised to get tested to see if we had the same condition. My test showed I had three valves.

2019 therefore finished on a very sad note. Mum was always very supportive, although she couldn't quite understand why, at my age, I wanted to take on this running challenge. She did think I was crazy!

Data wise, 2019 finished with 140 runs and 765 miles. I hadn't monitored the mileage in the years since I started the diary in 2003, but I would be very surprised even in the two years I ran marathons if I had run more miles than 765.

140 runs in the year was also a 'personal best' surpassing my only previous three figure years - 100 runs in 2005 and 113 in 2010.

Another PB was seven half marathons in a year, beating three in 2005. Throw in a parkrun PB and taking part in 26 other organised events, and 2019 was a somewhat transformational year for my running.

None of us though had any idea that a massive disrupter was going to hit us in 2020.

3.
IS THIS REALLY HAPPENING?

I returned from that Jim Lawless business event thinking 'Have I really done this? Have I really just announced that in two and a bit years' time I'm going to run 44 miles, when right now a half marathon would feel like a big challenge?'

I think it took two or three months to embed itself as an idea that I was actually going to go ahead and carry through on what I had announced – how many times in life and business have you met people who have seemingly on the spur of the moment come up with ideas and suggestions that sound very challenging, but ultimately they fade away or they start something and then it stops?

I remember when I launched my business podcast in March 2018 someone telling me that the average podcast only got as far as episode seven, because by then the momentum had gone, the ideas had started to dry up and it was just easier to stop than to keep on trying to make it happen.

So I was very conscious that I didn't want this to be one of those situations, where I had got the applause for the idea but then allowed it to drift away and not happen.

So I did three things:

Firstly, I came up with the 'branding' of 44@60 - don't ask how or why, it just happened. I'm sure you've experienced that with your own business branding. The 'lightbulb' moment as some call it. 44@60 sort of said everything about what I was planning to do. 44 miles at the age of 60.

Secondly, I had a page created on my website where I could record my progress - essentially a log of my training runs, but with opportunities to add how I was feeling and how I felt the whole thing was going. This was important because it was evidence that the idea was moving forward. It was also a great way of convincing myself that I was going to see this through.

Thirdly, I launched a podcast. Called initially '44@60' before becoming 'Running 44@60'. More on the podcast later, but in itself it was a hugely valuable motivation and learning tool. I started interviewing those who had run the Classic Quarter, those who knew about running and those who offered advice and tips for eating, kit, shoes, etc...

'I BOUGHT A HYDRATION VEST - I WAS BECOMING AN ULTRA RUNNER'

I was starting to think of myself as a runner. A potential ultra runner. I was getting into the 'zone'. And of course every time a podcast episode went 'live', that created momentum and made the whole thing feel as though it was continually moving forward.

I talked to people at the running club, I talked to my friends, indeed I began to take every opportunity to let people know that this was what I was planning to do and in the 'Shouting' section I explain how that took on a whole new level of 'yes this is really happening'.

IS THIS REALLY HAPPENING TO US?

As with the running once you've set your business goal or BHAG it needs to feel real.

So tell everyone about it. Your team, your suppliers, even your customers.

Set up innovative ways of monitoring activity, ideas and successes.

And if you are, as I am, a one-person business, there are going to be lots of times when you think 'Is this really me? Am I really capable of this? Will that large company really want to work with me?'

As I write this book, I'm thinking 'Is this really me - am I really writing and publishing a business book?'

In all walks of business life, even the most outwardly confident people do have self-doubt from time to time, on the inside, and it's very easy to talk ourselves out of things.

How many times have you thought of a new way of offering your product or service, or indeed a new product or service or ideas to break into a new market, and yet somehow it never actually happens usually because you talk yourself out of it?

I remember reading somewhere that they say 'in life you don't regret the things you do, only the things you don't or didn't do', and I think that very much applies to business.

You've got a good idea to do things differently or get on the radar of a company you would like to work with. Or you say to yourself - 'Yes I should get in touch with that person'.

When that happens, you need to do it and you need to do whilst you've got momentum, because momentum in business is vital to success.

Proposed actions and ideas can quickly dissipate. How many times have you been to a conference or event like the one I went to, and you are listening to a speaker who shares an idea, and you think 'that's a great idea we need to do that', but then it never happens?

You get back to your business and it feels just too tricky to make it happen and so you take the easy option and just continue as you are.

The exciting bit happens when you do decide to go ahead. That is when you can get that sense of energy and excitement that you wouldn't normally experience.

Sometimes, of course, circumstances force us to make things happen differently, and a classic example obviously has been the pandemic, where for a number of businesses, mine included, the pandemic forced us to do things that we had often thought about doing but for various reasons hadn't.

I joke that pre COVID I had a Zoom paid account for two years and had probably used it twice.

Suddenly like lots of others I was having to learn how to use Zoom (other virtual software programmes are available). I started recording podcasts on Zoom.

A sales coaching day that I had been hired to deliver, for a group of new businesses was cancelled, but then the organisers asked, 'could I deliver it virtually?' - I immediately said yes even though I had never done that before.

Suddenly I was doing stuff in a way that was new to me. But it was happening.

So if you want to make something happen, then you need to give it some momentum, to be serious about it and to avoid too many conversations with too many people who will tell you it's a ridiculous idea that will never happen.

What's that theory about surrounding yourself with like-minded people, people who will encourage you to make your idea happen rather than those who will just focus on drumming into your head that it can't possibly happen.

Of course, we all need a dose of reality, but maybe that reality comes when we have given something a go and it hasn't worked out. But let's not *not* give something a go just because the people we associate with think it's a poor idea. That would have killed the vast majority of innovations!

'MAKE THINGS HAPPEN - BE PROACTIVE AND BELIEVE IN WHAT YOU ARE DOING'

So if you've got an idea for something and you really are keen to make it happen, then do everything in your power to make it happen.

You do need the planning, the preparation, the business plan, etc., and if you do all that it will also help you make it feel real.

When I decided I was going to write this book, I immediately started to write it, because I knew that unless I took some action I would forget about it, or not do it, or just think it was too much of a task and I wasn't capable of creating this book.

It would have been very easy to talk myself into thinking 'Who is going to be interested, who really wants to know about my 44@60 and the business lessons that I think I've learnt?'

And that's another thing that very often we overlook. No doubt as a reader of this book, there is an aspect of business which you are very good at and very knowledgeable at, because that's what you've been doing for a period of time.

It would be very easy to think that your knowledge and expertise is of no real value because you assume everybody else has got the same knowledge and expertise. Well the fact is that usually they haven't!

One of my business skills and experiences is presenting. I've got to the stage where I really look forward to it and I'm probably not bad at it, but I have to remember that whilst I may look forward to presenting and I may feel confident about doing it, the vast majority of people aren't in that boat.

They are the ones who don't look forward to presenting, they don't feel confident about doing it, and would really rather do anything else than stand up to a live or virtual audience and deliver a presentation. If you are a service provider in the business sector, then never assume that whatever it is you're going to offer is something everybody already knows about and is very good at.

So let's make a pledge to make things happen.

If you've got that really good business idea, then do whatever it takes to get it out there, put it on your website, talk to people about it when you go networking, and as such be confident of your ability to deliver it.

And yes, there will be times when you think 'Is this really me? Can I really do that?'

Only relatively recently I got a call from a person I'd never heard of, working for a brand I *have* heard of, who at quite short notice wanted some help for some of his colleagues to deliver key presentations to various investors around the globe.

And he asked me if I thought I would be able to work with them. After asking several questions about what exactly they were hoping to achieve by working with someone like me, I said 'Yes I can do that' and was hired.

I found out later that one of the reasons I was hired was because the video on my website of me explaining my service came across well, as did the way I asked lots of questions about what the expectations were around working with the team.

If you have a business or are thinking about starting one then turning your ideas into reality can be the tough part.

You'll find loads of reasons not to make things happen.

And then it's your call.

You give up the idea.

Or you make it happen.

Come on you can do it.

You can make it happen.

SECTION SUMMARY - TOP BUSINESS TIPS: MAKE IT HAPPEN

- Visualise what it will be like when your idea happens
- Take action to make it happen
- Tell people what you're doing
- Don't let doubts put you off
- Find people who will be positive and encouraging
- Don't be put off by those who suggest it's not a great idea or find faults in your plan
- Learn from their input but turn their negatives into determined positives. You will prove them wrong!
- Be prepared to pivot from time to time
- You know you are capable of this
- If you don't give it a go, you'll never know what might have happened
- Remember, we often regret the things we didn't do rather than the things we did do

RUNNING DIARY; EARLY 2020

2020 began like any other running year. Having racked up 140 runs and 765 miles in 2019, clearly 2020 was going to be a year where I would almost certainly be doing more miles.

I had already planned to reduce the number of events I took part in, in order to be a lot more selective and ensure all runs were working towards the goal 18 months on, in June 2021.

I had, along with several other members of the Truro running club, entered the Manchester marathon in April, as it was relatively easy to get to because we could fly from Newquay and I had a Airbnb organised somewhere not far from the start.

I saw this as good preparation in my build up to running the Classic Quarter in June as a relay of two with my running friend Andy Williams. The relay of 2 means we run half each and it's an opportunity to get a feel for the event and the course etc...

The Manchester marathon was scheduled eight weeks before the Classic Quarter so a great opportunity to do a long run which was part training run and for me that 3rd marathon.

A bit of running work to do before then though so back to January 2020, and my running year began at the Land's End parkrun.

My cricket buddy Jim McKenna claims not to be a runner, but he was keen to attend the official opening of the Lands End parkrun as living in Penzance this was his nearest one. I picked him up, noting he hadn't any running kit with him.

He explained how important support spectators were to parkrun. They had started parkrun at Lands End the previous November but this was to be the grand opening with the 'ribbon' being cut by local hero and Olympic gold medallist Helen Glover.

The course was out and back, and then a couple of laps around one or two of the landmarks to get up to 5km. I recorded 25:13 which I was really pleased with, and as I write this it is my joint third fastest parkrun alongside Cardiff and behind two I did at Market Rasen racecourse up in Lincolnshire when visiting family.

The following day I ran 15 miles in just under three hours and according to my running diary that was the longest run I had done since the Eden marathon in October 2010. The road to long running had begun!

A week later I did 18 miles around the roads of Truro in three hours 16 minutes.

I travelled to Lincolnshire for my mothers funeral and did a 10k which I done many times over the years, known as the Barkwith block.

It was a route that I had first done when I was a kid on a bike with my mates and I've been running it regularly, certainly since I started the running diary back in 2003.

According to my running diary I clocked 55:35 that day, and further research showed that six years earlier, in January 2014 when I had been in Barkwith for my father's funeral, I had done 55:13.

Not too bad losing just 22 seconds over six years. My 'course' PB was 47:34 which I had done on my 52nd birthday in 2013 – which was the last time I was up there for my actual birthday.

My mother, I'm sure, would have been proud of my ultra run achievement even though she would have thought I was crazy, and she would have worried about me not dropping dead on the course.

The day after my mother's funeral, my son Jim, who was up from Brighton Medical School for the funeral, joined me on the Market Rasen parkrun on the Saturday.

I think it was his first. I did 24:55, which is my second fastest and he did 25:53. He's since become a more regular runner. I suspect I'll not beat him again anytime soon at a parkrun!

I did a 15 miler at the beginning of February alongside the usual parkruns and club nights. On the 16th I did the Bodmin half which I noted was very tough and was reflected in my time of 2:17.

On the last day of February, which that year was the 29th, I did an event called the Classic Jack - (no relation to the Classic Quarter) organised by Dave and the Bys Vyken events team.

Dave creates some iconic races along fabulous routes supported by his infamous race briefing notes! If you're not run a Bys Vyken race you need to!

This was my first experience of a coastal path run of more than the half marathon distance. We were bussed out from St Ives to the starting point at St Just before then heading back 18 miles to St Ives.

The coastal path was very slippery and very rocky, and I described it as my toughest run ever. At one point I stepped into a puddle that suddenly disappeared up to my knee!

Even with grippy shoes on, I found it virtually impossible to run, because it was so slippery, so whilst I enjoyed the experience I was pleased to cross the finish line!

Little did any of us know that this would be the last event we would take part in for several months. I finished in 5 hours 18 minutes. The longest run time wise I had completed. I was just pleased to be inside the six hour cut off.

Given what lay ahead, it was somewhat ironic that my 2020 running plans first started to change not because of the pandemic that was COVID 19, but because regional airline FlyBe went bust. That happened mid-February, which meant the flights to Manchester for the April marathon were no longer going to happen. I really didn't fancy driving up or indeed going in a mini-bus.

My decision to withdraw was confirmed for me when I checked the cancellation conditions for my AirBnB, to discover it had been de-listed in December. That news hadn't reached me, but the hosts and the system were very efficient in refunding my booking.

I would later be able to gain an event refund. At the time I decided to go back to what was my original plan for an April marathon - Newport. It was within driving distance and my daughter Bethany was in her last year at the Royal Welsh School of Music in Cardiff. As we all know, just around the corner was a huge change to all our lives.

By mid-March the world was changing significantly. What turned out to be our last club night before lockdown was on Wednesday, March 11th. I did the local parkrun on the 14th, which was my 98th. I didn't expect to have to wait 16 months to get to my hundred!

On the 20th my daughter and son, Bethany and Jim, returned from different universities within a few minutes of each other. Parkrun was now suspended, so I did my own in a local park, recording a podcast along the way.

I think, like most people at that stage we thought that this was going to be something that might last a few weeks, possibly a couple of months.

On Monday the 23rd, the UK Prime Minster, Boris Johnson, announced to the nation that non-essential businesses would close, and that as citizens we weren't allowed out unless it was for essential shopping or to complete our daily exercise allowance.

The following day I started a new route which took me to the village shop in Playing Place, just south of Truro. I would run about three miles to the shop, fill up my hydration vest with all sorts of essentials, including for my neighbour the local West Briton newspaper and then run about two-and-a-bit miles back via a different route.

Like a few people I knew the restriction of being allowed one exercise time outdoors per day became a combination of an instruction and a challenge. I ran eight successive days at the start of lockdown. That boosted my March tally to 19 runs and 108 miles – both personal bests for a calendar month.

As we now know these lockdown conditions continued for a significant amount of time. I did get into a routine of doing my own version of parkrun on a Saturday, starting from my house and trying to find a different course each time including one where I ran 18 laps of a local grass space quite close to where I live.

I set myself a goal of making sure that I finished every single one of them in under 30 minutes. I also started each 'not a parkrun' at the normal start time of 9am on a Saturday.

The other thing that happened was that Bethany and Jim got into running as well, having not really done too much previously. It was something we could do together and one of the only opportunities to be allowed out of our house.

I did another 19 runs in April and this time 122 miles, with the longest run being on Sunday the 26th of April. That was the date of the cancelled London Marathon. The organisers created the 26 Challenge Day as a virtual substitute. The idea was to do a run which featured 26. You could run for 26 minutes or 26 miles or any distance or time that involved 26 or a 2 and a 6. I decided to run for 2.6 hours, which is two hours 36 minutes, and I covered 14.3 miles.

Training for an ultra marathon I learnt was not all about running long distances. As with any training programme you need variety. 'Not a parkrun' offered the opportunity to run at high intensity for just under 30 minutes and this was added to when and Jim and I started doing a 10k time trial.

We started near what was then the football ground in Truro, joined the old tram line, the Newham trail, just past County Hall, ran to its end on Gas Hill, turned right along Newham road, went round the turning circle at the road's end then retraced our steps with at the end a hurtle down a small park and the final stretch back to our house.

It got quite competitive as we went all in. As with parkrun I couldn't see the point of dawdling along. This was after all a time trial and we were racing each other and the clock!

I did win the first couple but then Jim got into his stride and apart from the odd occasion he did tend to win relatively easily.

Bethany decided in June she would run her own and her first half marathon, so we spent time in May plotting a course, whilst keeping the not-a-parkrun going on a Saturday on different routes from the front door, as well what was known known as the Playing Place Thursday morning paper shop run.

The miles were racking up, even though there were no running club meet ups and all events were cancelled, including the Classic Quarter in June.

As the summer reached its height, and some easing of restrictions were on the horizon the Classic Quarter organisers announced that they were targeting early September for the event. My relay of 2 with Andy Williams was back on! That was a great motivator to keep on racking up the training miles.

Bethany and I ran her half marathon in around two hours 45 minutes, which was great because the target was to be under three hours. A number of her friends around the country did their own versions on their own courses. Virtual 'races' were in full swing as a way of keeping runners motivated.

So by the time we reached the halfway point of 2020 my running had been consistent. I was mixing up the distances and the pace. I was in reasonable shape.

By the end of June, I was up to 582 miles for the year and had completed 91 runs, easily on target to beat my 2019 record of 745 miles and 140 runs.

COVID 19 was causing huge disruption and devastation across the world. Lives were being lost, the NHS was under severe pressure, many people were off work on the furlough scheme. Those that were working were being advised to work from home. We clapped for the NHS and we wore masks.

Lots of massive downsides.

But for me some upsides.

Having Bethany and Jim at home for what would turn out to be almost six months was a huge bonus.

We did lots of running together that we would never have done, or indeed are ever likely to do again. Bethany finished her degree virtually - her final exam performance piece should have been in a grand hall with a big audience, and instead it was on Zoom in her bedroom.

We were amongst the lucky ones, though, there is no doubt about that.

If things returned to 'normal' of sorts in 2021 and the Classic Quarter happened at the beginning of June, I was now less than year away from the 44 mile challenge.

I had been lucky to stay injury free.

I had clocked up an average of almost 100 miles a month.

Despite everything my plan was on schedule.

4.

HOW AM I GOING TO DO THIS?

Preparation and planning. I think it was fairly obvious to me soon after I announced I was going to take on this challenge, that I had to be well organised. At the moment I said I was going to do it, I knew nothing about how to plan and prepare to run 44 miles.

I had run two marathons in 2005 and 2010 and on both occasions I had followed a training plan, but I learnt fairly early on as I started to research running 44 miles, that there was a lot more to it than just a training plan, from a running point of view.

I was clearly going to need to learn about covering a distance almost twice as far as I'd ever run before, and being on my feet way more than twice as long as I'd ever been before.

I needed to learn about eating and drinking on the run, organising a crew, achieving cut off times and getting my head round such a monumental distance.

When I announced that I was going to do the Classic Quarter, it was over two years away. I remember having conversations with people that summer who asked me when I was going to do the run. My reply 'well not until 2021', made it feel a long way off. Indeed, it turned out to be 815 days from announcement day to run day.

When the target date is a long way off you can easily park it and think, ‘I don't need to do anything about that for ages yet’ and then of course that ‘ages yet’ creeps up on you.

‘I KNEW NOTHING ABOUT RUNNING 44 MILES’

One piece of preparation I did have was the running diary, which I had started in November 2003, and in which I had recorded every single outdoor run since then, so that was a bit of a head start in terms of preparation and planning.

Another key thing I had to learn was to time the training. There was little point, in that first year of 2019, thinking I was going to be doing regular 20 mile runs.

In a sense it was like the principle of Olympic athletes. You spend an awful lot of time trying to ensure that you peak on a particular day, which at the time you started your preparation could be four years away.

So I created what was largely a very loose plan, and that was to use 2019 to up my running and learn from other runners, particularly experienced ultra runners and those who had run the Endurancelife Classic Quarter.

On my agenda were a couple of other off-road events, starting in 2019 with an 11 mile race on the coastal path (the White Rat) which is detailed in section 2, and then in early 2020 the 18 mile event between St Just and St Ives.

I think the big thing that helped me in terms of the planning and preparation was to set a target of running in 2020 the event as a relay of two, because that in itself, in 2019, felt like a very big challenge indeed. The relay of two was simply running half the course and then handing over to a team-mate who ran the second half.

And yes, I did consider that one of the potential downsides of that would be that I found running half of it so hard that it would feel impossible to contemplate 12 months later running the entire route. As a footnote, that actually did happen! The relay of two was delayed by COVID to September 2020, and to make the run as safe as possible the handover points for the relay of four and the relay of two were changed. I ran the first half, which was extended by the changes to 25.7 miles - which as someone pointed out later, was only half a mile short of completing a marathon. At the time of the 'handover' to my team-mate Andy Williams, I do recall thinking 'how on earth can I run another 20 miles?'

Another facet to my plan was to run various sections of the course in advance of the actual event.

I did the first one of those in August 2019, when I did an out and back of about five miles of the course, and I was planning in 2020 to run the whole thing in about four or five different sections from around April onwards, but that was ended as a plan by the pandemic situation.

Nearer the time of the relay, I did some detailed planning of the route, including mapping it out, as well as watching video clips of various parts of it and learning from previous runners who came on the Running 44@60 podcast.

The podcast ultimately was a huge source of ideas and tips for planning and preparation and is covered in more detail in the section six called 'Learning'.

BUSINESS PLANNING

There's an old, much quoted, phrase by Benjamin Franklin: 'If you fail to plan, you are planning to fail'.

Whenever I work with clients in the business world, whether that's helping them grow sales or deliver better presentations, I relentlessly bang on about the need to prepare, to plan and to practice, and all of those three played a big part of my 44@60 campaign.

If you are going after a BHAG, planning will be fundamental to success, and in business at all levels we often do fail to plan properly, and then wonder why we didn't succeed.

Planning at a business level ranges from an annual business plan to a plan to gain a new customer, or make the most of a networking event, or move premises, or use new technology.

One of the guests on my podcast was Anna Pascoe, a specialist long distance runner who also has a business called 'Make me a Plan'. Anna kindly created for me a plan for the three weeks leading up to the run, around rest, eating and staying run-ready.

In my experience not enough businesses spend enough time planning.

Has your company got a business plan?

Sometimes you can end up spending too much time on the planning. During my business career, working in the media sector we had to present a business plan every year to those who had responsibility for our overall group, based in an office in London.

Each centre, of which we were one of about 15, was required to construct and then present a business plan for the following financial year, in quite significant detail. During the presentation we would be questioned and potentially challenged by the 'London team' who were responsible ultimately for the 15 centre plans coming together as a collective success.

It undoubtedly became a bit of a game.

The rules of the game were simple:

You had to produce a plan that got approval but which was ultimately achievable, indeed if you were too defensive then you would be asked to produce more and if you were too bold you would be challenged for being too ambitious.

Usually the plans for the financial year ahead were signed off around two to three months before that year actually started, so almost inevitably the plan would quickly be out of date. Not dramatically, but usually in its make-up of the overall target, which meant that every three months the plan was checked and potentially revised. At local level we were always keen to try and revise it downwards rather than upwards – to give ourselves the best chance of achieving it!

I think the point here is that you have to have a business plan if you are going to set yourself any sort of target, whether that be a Big, Hairy, Audacious Goal target, or simply a target to do better than you did last year, or a target that ultimately means you stay in business.

Having a plan also makes the target feel more achievable. Those business plans that I mentioned above were exactly that. You are ultimately pursuing a revenue target that looks enormous. So what you do is break it down into various types of revenue stream and then those streams themselves will be further broken down into products and subcategories, and then you break it down again by month and week.

It simply means you have to achieve X amount per product in a subcategory per week for a full year and that was repeated across all the other subcategories.

The point I'm trying to make is that the key to achieving what looks like a pretty daunting target is to break it down into small parts, because it then feels much more achievable.

'HAVING A BUSINESS PLAN WILL ELEVATE YOUR SELF-STATUS'

And that's what I did with the run. I never thought of it in terms of planning to run 44 miles, I thought of it as 15 three-mile sections. I knew I was well capable of running three miles so all I had to do was repeat that a total of 15 times.

And that is the way I would advise you to think when you are doing your business planning.

Break your goal down into manageable chunks that look like the sort of things you and your team are already achieving.

And as with the run, start to do the planning as soon as you have effectively set the goal, and keep the planning momentum going. There will be changes on the route to your goal, but they will be much easier to implement if you already have the plan flowing.

And having that plan and sharing it with your colleagues, your team, your business connections, your family, your customers, will, as it did with the run, start to help you convince yourself that this is all possible.

As I've already mentioned, often in business we get excited about the potential plan, but that excitement wears off very quickly, we lose momentum and end up coming up with all sorts of reasons and excuses for not then pursuing our goal.

Don't let that happen to you. Set your goal. Create your plan to achieve it, and tell everybody what you going to do.

But be prepared to pivot that plan because inevitably certain things beyond your control will change; witness the dramatic effect the pandemic had on business plans across the globe, from its start in early 2020.

That's where the realism of business planning kicks in. For most businesses, their 2020 plans were massively disrupted as they were forced to close, or place some of their team on furlough and adapt to working from home.

It is unlikely that any business would have planned for what happened.

Most, though, found themselves planning around an environment and conditions they had never experienced before. If your business was one of those, then try and find the positives from that 'emergency' planning.

Who knows, some of the things you were forced to do differently may well turn out to be things you will benefit from, things you might not have changed had you not been forced to.

Finally I often hear people say 'my business isn't big enough to have or need a business plan.'

I disagree.

I think, regardless of the size of your business, having a business plan is a good idea.

If you've never had a business plan before, then start with something quite modest in terms of content. And then add to it. You will find quite quickly that your plan starts to grow in terms of its details. The other thing that will happen is that having a business plan can start to make you feel much more like a business. That might sound a little odd but lots of people running businesses, especially one man / one woman businesses, often don't think of themselves as 'proper' businesses or indeed 'proper' businesspeople.

We talked about 'self doubt' in an earlier section. Having a business plan will give you more confidence and without doubt will help grow your business, if that is what you want to do.

I'm a one person business, but ever since I set up in 2012, I've put together an annual business plan.

It includes the services I offer and plan to offer, how they will be delivered, and the fees associated with them. I then set targets for each service, in terms of how many I want to 'sell'. Some simple maths then gives me a target revenue. Add in some details of your likely costs, including how much you pay yourself, and you have a profit target.

I have no doubt that I would not have achieved my running goal without a series of plans. Everything from training, through to eating and drinking, to where and when on the route I was going to meet my crew, and what was going to happen when we did meet.

So if you haven't got one - get yourself a business plan!

SECTION SUMMARY - TOP BUSINESS TIPS: PLANNING

- Have you got a Business Plan?

- If yes how often do you check it, review it and potentially revise it?

- You should do that review once every three months or once a quarter to use business terminology

- Check what your plan contains - is there enough detail? There might be too much detail. If an outsider, say a business advisor or consultant, were to read your plan would they have a fair understanding of what your business was about and hoping to achieve?

- If you haven't got a business plan, then create one

- It doesn't need to be over elaborate or complicated

- Include the following:

- Revenue Streams and Sales Targets (inc Phasing)
- Key People - internal and external
- Cost Bases
- Customer Personas
- Timescales
- Production and Suppliers
- Marketing
- Distribution and Wholesalers

RUNNING DAIRY; MID 2020

As the second half of the year began some things started to return to 'normal'. For example, you could book a car parking spot and run round the grounds at the National Trust property at Trelissick where I had done the parkrun on many occasions prior to lockdown.

In the period from the March 23rd lockdown to the end of May there was a point where I'd run 260 miles whilst driving my car on two short journeys for a total of less than 30 miles. Looking back that period does seem somewhat surreal.

During July I did a couple of 10 to 11 mile runs around Trelissick. It's a great place to run as the woodland trails border the Fal river and there are a couple of woods to run through as well. One tip I would pass on as your training runs get longer, is to try and choose routes where time passes.

Some of you reading this may have used a treadmill. If you're anything like me, and note I'm fortunate enough to have a treadmill at home, you will know how hard it is to run on a treadmill for even 30 minutes.

And it's not the actual running for 30 minutes that is hard, it's the monotony of the treadmill. How people run beyond 30 minutes I'm not sure. A friend of mine recently told me that in preparation for a marathon, she did three and a half hours in a cross trainer in a gym. Three and a half hours!

Running outside is different. There are distractions. People, views, weather, ground conditions etc. anything that gives variety to your training will make it more enjoyable and make it feel like the time is passing.

For me, somewhere like Trelissick was a great place to build what I call 'time on feet'. Whilst I'm measuring distance covered and uploading it to Strava, ultimately these runs were as much about building the time I was running, rather than my speed.

I was still doing the Thursday morning paper run and the Saturday not-a-parkrun. That was important because when you are training for a long distance run, you need variety. Building up the stamina on the long runs but running the shorter ones at a faster pace. A speedy parkrun or some hill reps are all part of ultramarathon preparation.

Lockdown got lifted a bit in August as the UK Government launched the 'Eat out to help out' scheme, designed to save the hospitality industry by giving us all £10 off when we ate out. When lockdown was back in place in the autumn, there were suggestions that this scheme probably played a part. Enough of that though as this book isn't about politics!

The most significant announcement, for me, in early August, was that the Classic Quarter 2020 was going to go ahead on September 5th. Andy Williams and I confirmed that we would be doing the relay of two.

During lockdown, Truro running club had also started lots of virtual events - some as part of teams, others for solo runners. They were a great motivator to get out running and undoubtedly helped me prepare for the relay of two.

I note from my running diary that I didn't do that much long distance mileage in the build-up. The longest I ran was 13 miles on a coastal path route on the north coast of Cornwall, with a small group from the running club. Those were the days when small running groups were allowed.

On September 5th the Endurancelife Classic Quarter did take place. I ran the first leg starting at 7:02 am. Andy and myself 'crewed' for each other. This gave us some 'crewing' experience. Not only in terms of what we needed to do but also we got a feel for the best places for it.

If you are inspired to run an ultramarathon, having crew is a big help. I cover this in more detail in a later section but simply knowing you have support on the course is really valuable.

I probably carried too much food and drink, and indeed gave Andy far too much to top me up than was ultimately needed.

Our first meeting point was on Praa Sands beach about 18 miles into the run. Andy came enthusiastically over to me as I was making my way across the sand. He had the small rucksack I had filled with food and drink.

'What do you need?' he asked.

Apparently apart from a change of water bottle, I asked for a specific flavour of gel and two Jaffa cakes. He found it highly amusing that firstly, my requests were so specific and secondly, that he had to rummage through a fully laden rucksack in search of that one specific variety of gel.

We had a lot of fun recalling that in the Running 44@60 podcast episode we recorded the following day.

My 'half' of 44 miles had turned into 25.7 miles which took me 5 hours and 53 minutes. That was easily longer than I had ever run before.

Overall the event was very well organised and we were fortunate to have a good run in decent weather. We did okay overall and I think we finished in about ten and a half hours as a team of two, with Andy racing through the second half.

A good result and experience for us that gave us plenty of things to consider for the following year, certainly for me. I was hoping to try and persuade Andy that he should do the whole thing as well, which he did, racing round the whole course in 2021 in roughly the same time we had done as a relay of two.

As the pubs and restaurants were now open, we met up with several of the Truro Classic Quarter participants that evening to reminisce on our adventures. I remember talking to a couple of the runners who had done the full 44 miles. They were much better and younger runners than me and I remember them saying how tough it had been.

I declined the opportunity to go to a house party, and as I walked home I began to think about 2021 -it was now beginning to feel very real and even more scary!

The relay of two had meant I'd run further in time than ever before. I had completed almost the equivalent of a marathon on the ups and downs of the coastal path. I reflected on the fact that in less a year from then I was going to have run around 19 more miles. I was tired but, as I've discovered after long runs, whilst your legs are aching your brain is buzzing. I eventually fell asleep thinking about what lay ahead in 2021.

The next day Andy and I re-met on Zoom to record an episode of the Running 44@60 podcast recalling our adventure, and sharing our tips and advice. We were talking as though we were seasoned ultra runners, even though technically neither of us had yet run one!

What of course none of us realised at that point was that there would be a second wave of the pandemic, and this brief interlude in August and early September wouldn't last in terms of the shackles being released.

At the end of September I was able to go and visit my son in Brighton and catch up with a couple of friends, but by the beginning of October, lockdown two was kicking in and that was the end of small group running and any events as we all moved across the country into various tiers.

We had been very lucky that the Classic Quarter had gone ahead. Given the circumstances, the organisers - Endurancelife - did a superb job in my view.

Their master stroke, which I guess was somewhat forced upon them, was having individual start times.

On an event such as this, I think this is the way forward. It meant no jostling for position at the beginning, no inevitable early hold ups as the path narrowed, and no going off too fast to try and avoid the early hold ups.

Some would argue you don't get the feeling of a 'race', but let's face it, only a handful of the starters had any realistic chance of winning.

It was a great feeling to head off and only get overtaken a couple of times in the first few miles.

5.
SHOUTING

I read or heard somewhere once that if you want something to actually happen, you need to shout about it a lot. For this challenge it would have been very easy for me to have been listening to Jim Lawless, quietly decide I was going to do the Classic Quarter in 2021, but then as with many ideas, let the moment pass and allow the idea to be consigned to those that seemed great for a moment but were not followed through on.

So my shouting started straight away. I knew that when I had the chance to be introduced to the audience of around a 150 people, that if I didn't tell them I was going to run the event in 2021, there was a very good chance that I would talk myself out of it very quickly. But once I had gone public it would be increasingly difficult to do that, so it was without doubt a deliberate move on my part to seize the moment.

'IT BECOMES REAL WHEN YOU TELL EVERYONE ABOUT IT, ALL THE TIME'

And then once I had made the announcement, the challenge was to keep the ball rolling and to keep the momentum going, particularly as the Classic Quarter 2021 was at that point over 800 days away. Interestingly, in my running diary I note that that evening I went to club night as usual on a

Wednesday, but there is nothing in my running diary that says I made the big announcement earlier in the day!

I think the other two big moves that started to make it feel real were deciding to call it 44@60, and then in the summer, launching the 44@60 podcast.

The first episode of the podcast went out on 21 August 2019 and was simply called 'The journey to the 44 mile Classic Quarter in 2021 begins...' it was the shortest podcast I've ever recorded at seven minutes and 47 seconds, but somewhat ironically it was for a long time the most downloaded episode.

I started to have conversations with runners, simply because I was looking for people to come on the podcast and talk about it. I remember saying on many occasions 'ah yes the Classic Quarter - I'm running the whole thing in 2021.'

As I mention later on in the fundraising section the shouting got very much louder once we got actually into 2021, and in particular when I started to fundraise.

The 'shouting' then became an everyday occurrence, largely to promote the fundraising, and to try and attract people to come on the business masterclasses.

I made some home-made DIY signage for my shorts and my hydration vest, and if ever I was out on a run and people met me or said a word of encouragement, I would use the opportunity to slow down and tell them about 44@60.

Having said that, I can only recall one occasion where being out for a run and telling someone about it turned into a donation, and that was when I met someone I knew through business circles who I hadn't seen for a while.

The shouting bit that was without doubt most successful when I was business networking.

A few weeks after signing up with the Children's Hospice South West, they gave me the opportunity to attend their monthly business networking event as a speaker.

I had 15 minutes to talk about 44@60, and that did result in a few people signing up to the masterclass series as well as some additional personal donations.

I was fortunate to have one or two people in particular on the networking scene who were very good at helping promote what I was doing, and a shout out in this book in particular to Edward Chapman who himself is a seasoned ultra six-day runner. Edward not only supported the masterclasses but he also got me a gig to speak via Zoom at a running/business conference in South Africa, where I had 30 minutes to tell the story of 44@60.

That did result in some additional fundraising occurring, but more importantly it added to my momentum and belief that I could do this.

I am convinced that the decision taken over Christmas to raise £100 a mile for the Children's Hospice Musical Therapy programme gave both my training and my overall motivation a big boost at a crucial time, and gave me lots of excuses to do lots of shouting about what I was up to.

Small things also helped with the shouting, such as product placement! Every time I took part in any sort of virtual call or event, I had the Children's Hospice running vest on a hanger behind me, to the extent that whenever I logged into a call, or I was starting my own webinars, I would check the position of the vest and move it to ensure it got prime viewing position!

It gave people the opportunity to spot it and ask me about it.

I was also shooting little videos on my phone and posting them directly to the likes of LinkedIn to promote the fundraising webinars. I was using the webinars not only to raise money, but also to encourage those who were present to tell others about 44@60.

I have little doubt that the 'shouting' I did for 44@60 really boosted my overall confidence and the profile of my challenge. And it ensured that there was no opportunity to sneak away from the challenge! It had to happen!

The big lesson which I cover in the business section next up is that you have to be consistent in your shouting, in terms of the message and the frequency. It will feel relentless and there will be times when you think you're doing too much.

I remember listening to Janet Murray who has a very well-known business podcast. She was talking about email marketing and how often you should do it. The subject had arisen from one of her listeners suggesting that they were feeling uncomfortable about the frequency of their emailing activities. Janet's view was that once you start to feel uncomfortable about the frequency of your email marketing, then you are starting to head towards the point where you are getting closer to the frequency that you should be sending them!

And it's true. I found that I had to keep repeating the marketing message as a collective and to certain individuals, particularly those who said they would come on a programme but then didn't, those who said they would sponsor me but then hadn't.

The shouting bit is relentless!

WE CALL IT MARKETING, IN BUSINESS

In business we call it marketing rather than shouting, but essentially it's the same thing. You have a message that you want to get heard by an audience who you have identified as needing, or potentially needing, your product/service.

I've mentioned networking and I still believe that business networking is a great way of marketing yourself and your offering. I varied my networking on the basis that if I only went to the same networking group all the time, then sooner or later the story would start to sound a bit dull. By going to different networking events I met people for the first time and when I look back, a number of my sponsors were totally unknown to me at the beginning of the campaign.

One thing that worked really well and is something which I bang onto my clients to do, is to get yourself a 'gig' as an event speaker.

I created both a 15 and 30-minute version of 44@60 as a speaking gig, and having that captive audience to share the message with undoubtedly gave me lots of profile and boosted the fundraising.

Speaking is one of the easiest ways to get yourself and your product/service known, in my opinion. There are lots of networking events always looking for interesting speakers.

And there's the clue if you do get the opportunity to be a business event speaker.

What you deliver in your presentation needs to be interesting. And that is interesting to your audience, not necessarily to yourself!

So don't turn up and bang on about yourself, how great your product is, how many awards you have won, how proud you are of your sustainability plan, how big your coffee machine is, etc...

Instead tell a story that engages your audience. That's what I did.

I focused on the outcome - the benefit to the music therapy programme - and then weaved my way through the timeline from that seminal announcement moment to visualising what it was going to be like when I reached the finish line. The objective of my 'marketing' was to take the audience on my journey, to get them to feel what it would be like doing what I was planning to do, to understand the ups and downs, the emotions and challenges.

Marketing, and certainly speaking / presenting, is about sharing your knowledge and advice in a way that will benefit your audience.

If you do that, it will be far more memorable, and you are likely then to create a positive reaction in terms of getting on the radar, making new connections, starting conversations etc.

'IF NO ONE KNOWS ABOUT YOU, NO ONE IS GOING TO BUY FROM YOU'

Using various activities and actions to start conversations is, I think, fundamentally what marketing is all about. In most business scenarios, the beginning of the 'sale' is the initial conversation between the prospective buyer and seller.

A poster, a radio ad, a news or PR item, a sponsored social message, are all designed to get a conversation started and take it right through to a defined 'this is what we want you to do' message. (The call to action, or CTA in marketing speak.) This would be a mix of 'call us', 'visit us', 'message us', 'come along to...'. You know the sort of thing - although a lot of marketing has a jumbled or sometimes non-existent call to action.

Check the 'call to action' messages in your marketing!

To promote 44@60, I regularly sent out media news items on how I was doing. I think I probably ended up posting on LinkedIn virtually every day for three months prior to the event. I actually learnt a lot about Linked In during 44@60.

Regular posting is nothing new for those of you who are skilled marketeers, because you know that marketing is relentless. It's not something you can do occasionally. You have to do it all the time, and that in itself can be challenging particularly if your business doesn't have a marketing person.

I do know from working with several businesses that sometimes there is a fear that you over-shout, that people will get fed up of seeing your message.

I'm not sure that's true, because we are all bombarded every single minute of every single day with tons of marketing messages, probably more so than ever in our whole business careers. So if you're holding back, thinking 'I'll only send out an email once a month', or 'I'll only post on social media once a month' you are probably wasting an opportunity.

I know from the way my LinkedIn posts were interacted with that very few people saw all of them. Indeed, some of the reactions only happened a couple of weeks or even longer after I placed the post.

I do quite a bit of work with some of my clients on LinkedIn, and I suggest to them that they are proactive on it for just 10 minutes a day. By proactive I mean adding to your profile, sharing your ideas, reading other people's posts and both commenting on and sharing them.

But make sure when you do comment or share someone else's post that you that get noticed by them.

Avoid falling into the trap of taking the easy option which is clicking on the default comment buttons such as 'Congrats' or 'Well done'

Marketing whizzo Gary Vaynerchuk advocates making yours the best comment, because that will get you noticed.

He's right.

If you are trying to get on the radar of someone, then when they do post an article, be quick off the mark and make sure yours is one of the first comments to appear. But make it the best one, the one that is going to get their attention and prompt them to potentially reply. If they do reply - then guess what - a conversation has started.

My shouting about 44@60, certainly when I announced the fundraising, did feel utterly relentless, as I was seeking every single opportunity to tell as many people as possible about what I was doing and why I was doing it.

Finally let's talk investment.

My key investment in marketing 44@60 was time.

The time to create and post stuff.

The time to organise, create and deliver webinars.

The time to contact prospective supporters and sponsors personally.

You should do all of these.

You should also invest. You'll have heard this marketing story before - it goes something like this - the marketing guru addressing his/her audience asks everyone who has heard of Coca Cola to raise their right arm. Then raise their left arm if they've also heard of McDonalds.

Chances are everyone has both arms up. 'In that case', asks the marketing guru, 'why, when everyone has heard of them, are they amongst the biggest spending advertisers in the world?'

You could ask your business similar questions. Have all your prospective customers heard of you? The likelihood is the answer is no. In which case how will they get to hear about you?

Through marketing.

And through marketing in the right places.

Which means making the most of the 'free' opportunities, as well as investing in the best paid-for opportunities.

SECTION SUMMARY - TOP BUSINESS TIPS: MARKETING

- Marketing is identifying potential customers, getting your message to them and ensuring they enjoy a great customer experience when they respond and interact with you

- Be clear about your message and the actions you want it to create

- Ensure your marketing message is consistent across all platforms, from your website to your social media channels, and everything in between

- To be successful, your marketing needs to have a relentless approach

- That means an investment of both time and money

- Pick the marketing platforms where your prospective buyers are - these might be different to your personal preferences

- If marketing is free, is it really worth it?

- If you've got a website, ensure it clearly articulates what your offer is and why I, as a prospective customer, should be interested

- Make sure also that your website content is up to date

- Be wary of buying 'special offer' marketing

RUNNING DIARY; END OF 2020

After the Classic Quarter relay of two at the beginning of September, I did not-a-parkrun number 21 and then took part in a running club trial. Lockdown had eased and running club Wednesday nights were about to re-start.

During lockdown, the club had maintained member interest and motivation by organising a series of 'Captain's Challenges'. Members became part of virtual teams and the challenges varied. The one at the end of September included a 5am to 8am challenge. Simply how many miles you could run in that time.

I decided that was the one for me, working on the basis that a combination of the start time and running length would have others selecting from the September challenge menu different options.

I planned the flattest route I could find close to home. Essentially an out and back four-and-a-bit mile course. I completed 17.6 early morning miles, which earned me third spot. I had assumed this challenge would include an age handicap element, as many of the others had done. It didn't. Nevertheless, it was somehow enjoyable even if it was back and forth along the dual carriageway between Truro Football Club and Truro College. I started in darkness with hardly any vehicles on the road and finished in sunshine with vehicles in full Saturday morning mode.

Like many thousands of others, I missed Saturday morning parkruns. Having stumbled across parkrun at the beginning of 2017 I had become a huge fan. When we went into lockdown in March 2020, I had notched up 98 parkruns. My plan had been to run my 100th on the Saturday nearest to my birthday at the beginning of April, running in full cricket gear including bat, helmet, pads etc...

Why cricket gear?

Cricket is my main sport and a hundred in cricket is a big individual landmark / achievement.

Parkrun would return on July 24th 2021 - 497 days after the last one before lockdown. So on July 31st 2021 I got to my 100, and yes, I did go round in full cricket gear.

I was expecting to be right at the back so was delighted to do a sub-35 minute run - my 'usual' time for Trelisssick parkruns is 27-28 minutes.

On November 4th 2020 we had our last club run before lockdown 2, which began the day after. It meant, as we ran round Truro we were given a light show of fireworks, as residents held firework parties before the new lockdown kicked in.

Running could still happen. You could run on your own or with one other person.

At the beginning of December Cornwall was placed in a 'tier' that meant we could run in groups of six. The club set up a booking system on EventBrite. Runs were 'released' on a Sunday evening and it became very competitive between us run leaders as to who would 'sell out' first.

Initially as run leaders we had to book ourselves on to the runs we were leading. The flaw in that became apparent when I tried to book onto my own run to discover it was already full!

I do think people had more Christmas lights on display than usual, to try and add some cheer to the Lockdown experience, so we organised runs on club nights around the best lights.

My mileage ticked over in the final quarter of 2020. An average of 12 runs and nearly 90 miles per month.

I finished 2020 with a total of 159 runs - a PB - and 1,105 miles - another PB.

Previous 'PBs' had been 140 runs and 745 miles in a calendar year.

I took part in just three organised races, including the Classic Quarter relay of two compared with 26 organised races in 2019.

Lockdown in 2020 was hugely disruptive to everyone's lives. For runners the things we took for granted - club nights, parkruns, events etc...all changed.

There were however some upsides which without lockdown would not have happened. I was one of the lucky ones and my list of running 'upsides' may well be longer than that of most people.

Here are my lockdown running upsides:

- Eight successive days of running after lockdown was first announced - I had never run on more than 3 successive days before.

- My children returning from university and staying all spring and summer, during which time they both got into running.

- My daughter Bethany and I planned and ran together her first ever half marathon.

- Running 'not-a-parkrun' every Saturday from home and planning a different 'front door to front door' route. This became a regular routine and one of those semi-addictive running sequences you try not to break. Mine had a break after around 18 weeks when I had 10 days off running to settle a groin strain.

- Running to Playing Place shop early every Thursday, filling up the hydration vest with essentials and running back. Five miles in total. I became quite well known in the shop. Since lockdown ended I have never run this route.

- Enjoying the 'group of six' club runs which proved a great way to get to know more running club members and support each other.

As 2020 ended it was confirmed that the 2021 Endurancelife Classic Quarter would be on May 22nd, 142 days away. That was suddenly feeling quite close.

Remarkably it was already 673 days since I had made that announcement at that business event.

Had I made best use of those 673 days?

Was I at the place I needed to be, training and preparation wise, with less than five months to go?

Despite the disruption of 2020 I felt I was on schedule. Plenty of runs, lots of mileage.

Bring on 2021.

Let's just hope the Classic Quarter goes ahead as planned.

6.
LEARNING

When I announced that I was going to take on this challenge, I knew absolutely nothing about how to prepare, plan and eventually run 44 miles.

However, one of the things I have always been good at throughout my career is tapping into the experience, expertise, advice and ideas of others and I certainly did this in the time leading up to the event itself.

I bought several ultra running books, which is a very inexpensive way of learning how to run an ultramarathon. These are listed in the appendix section.

I launched the Running 44@60 podcast, which I mentioned in the shouting section. The podcast gave me the opportunity to learn about long distance running and about the Classic Quarter itself. I am indebted therefore to those who were prepared to come on the podcast as a guest, in order to share their tips and to give me the opportunity to ask them lots of searching questions. They are listed in the 'Thanks' section at the end.

There are also lots of people that I met in the running club, as well as at the events I took part in in 2019, who tolerated me firstly telling them all about my plans for 2021, and then when they revealed they had some ultra running experience, putting up with me asking them lots of questions about it!

The 44@60 podcast launched on August 21st 2019. It was simply an eight minute episode called 'The journey to the 44 mile Classic Quarter in 2021 begins' – I was full of imagination when it came to naming podcast episodes!

I had at that stage been producing a business podcast every Monday for well over a year, so I did have some experience of podcasting.

After recording episode two on the run whilst taking part in the 11 mile Roseland August Trail (RAT), my first interview was with seasoned runner Andy Goundry.

At that stage I hadn't considered using Zoom as a podcast interview tool - that really only happened when we went into the first lockdown in March 2020. So I turned up at Andy's office with my recording machine.

I plugged in a microphone for each of us, switched on and then realised that nothing was being recorded. I checked the machine, and to my horror discovered that I hadn't inserted an SD recording card.

Fortunately I remembered that in the indoor market in Truro, which was about a five minute jog from Andy's office, there was a guy who sold SD cards. I legged it down the street into the market and returned, blowing hard, to do the interview.

That was a lesson in making sure that you get your preparation right!

In those early days I was lugging equipment around to people's houses, their offices, to the running club, to cafes etc. and literally sitting face-to-face with them to do a recording. When during the pandemic that couldn't happen, I was forced to learn how to use Zoom as a tool for recording podcasts. It was so much easier!

The topics covered, apart from the actual Classic Quarter event itself, included eating and drinking, stretching, hill work, preparation and planning, as well as the more technical parts of ultra running such as pace, walking up hills, using poles, organising a crew and the mental side of a long-distance run.

If you are planning your own ultra run then there are lots of people who will be more than happy to share with you their advice and experience, and I would urge you to listen to them, to ask questions and to practice using their advice, particularly around eating and drinking.

Whenever you seek to learn, you have to also be a little bit selective, and pick the bits that are going to work for you. If I had taken with me everything that people suggested, in terms of eating for example, I would have needed a supermarket trolley to get it all in!

'I KNEW NOTHING ABOUT HOW TO RUN 44 MILES ON A COASTAL PATH'

So here is a summary of the key learning points for running an ultramarathon - particularly if it's your first one:

Tell other runners you're doing it and they will happily share their experiences. Listen to what they say. Take it all in.

Learn what works for you through practice. Starting from the bottom up - your shoes.

'Run the hills in training, walk them in the event' - sound advice given to me by one experienced ultra runner.

On the run, don't wait until you're thirsty before you drink, and don't wait until you're hungry before you eat. This is top advice, as is practising eating and drinking during your training. The aforementioned Andy Goundry told me that the Classic Quarter was more of an eating competition than a running one. I detail more about eating and drinking in section eight.

Don't end up as I did in that first half marathon, having to nip into a corner shop to buy a Mars bar - especially as corner shops are few and far between on coastal path runs.

I learnt to use running poles. I was told that in the UK most people don't use them but in other countries they are popular. I bought some that folded down into 4 sections and attached to either side of my hydration vest. There is a technique to using them.

Get it right and it does feel like you have a third leg, in particular when climbing steps. And there are a lot of steps on the Classic Quarter route. I also learnt to be patient when unfolding and re-folding them. I could just about get them out whilst still running, but I usually stopped at the top of an incline to fold them away.

That's something else I learnt. The odd minute or two spent re-folding poles isn't going to massively affect your finish time. Indeed, that minute or two stood still at the top of the hill is probably a good thing.

My advice - use poles - but practice using them.

Be hungry to learn.

It will be so helpful.

DO WE STOP LEARNING IN BUSINESS?

Whenever I deliver business webinars or masterclasses or workshops or indeed training programmes, I almost always refer to what I see as two of the biggest challenges in business.

They are simply:

- Keeping up with your customers
- Staying ahead of your competition

Keeping up with your customers has got harder in the last few years, as customers become more highly researched, more savvy about what's available, and as such less reliant on you to provide them with information. Indeed, I've seen it mentioned in several places that it is reckoned that in the business-to-business sector, around 70% of buying decisions are being made prior to any direct contact with the company that the customer wants to buy from.

So keeping up with our customers and potential customers means we have to keep learning, not just about our own products and services, but about the way our customer wants to access them, use them, buy them. We also need to be very knowledgeable about the sector we are operating in, because again, customers will be on top of that.

Staying ahead of our competitors means we need to be making the best use of the resources that are now available to us, particularly in terms of technology. As a business consultant, I work with numerous different organisations and individuals, and one of the common patterns that I see is a resistance to change based on a very outdated mantra: ‘if it ain't broken don't fix it’ - translated as ‘we’ve always done it like this, it seems fine, so why change?’

The problem with that attitude is that if we wait for things to be broken before we fix them, then we miss out. The business world around us is constantly innovating to enhance what is offered and improve products, services and processes, in terms of efficiency, ease of use and ultimately a better customer experience being delivered.

So the system you have been using for many years may well not be broken, but that is not an excuse not to look to improve it on behalf of your customers, because if you don't utilise what is now available, then there is every chance that your competitors will, and thus every chance that they will steal a march on you.

'IF YOUR BUSINESS IS TO GROW, YOU NEED TO KEEP LEARNING'

Just consider the way the business disruptors of recent years have utilised the benefits of technology to create not only new markets but to significantly impact on traditional ones.

If you are a runner reading this, you may well have taken part in a race which meant travelling and utilising/needing accommodation.

Have you tried to book a traditional B&B via a Google search? It's virtually impossible, mainly because the traditional B&B market was very slow to make booking easy, and that in my opinion is without doubt the big advantage AirBnB has: it is so easy to make a booking, change a booking, cancel a booking. It’s also not easy to find traditional B&B’s using a search engine as the front page listings are dominated by the booking agency type companies. And let’s face it how many of us ever turn to page two or page three of a Google search?

In business we have to keep learning, we need to keep utilising the advantages that technology provides and not using some poor excuse that the way we've always done it seems to be perfectly adequate.

The big learning lesson here is that it might well be perfectly adequate for you, but increasingly it will no longer be adequate for your customer, and certainly for your potential customer. You have to constantly put yourself in your customer's shoes not your own. Speak to them. Ask what they need from you and how they want to receive it. Some of course won't know what they want. Others will have a clear vision. Learning from our customers is something traditionally we've not been great at.

And I don't mean learning by sending out a survey. Who actually fills in a survey? And who fills in one properly? Incentives help, but are you getting genuine feedback or are you just receiving a survey completed as quickly as possible simply to enable its contributor to be entered into your prize draw?

The best way to learn from customers is to make that type of information gathering part of all interactions with the company at whatever level and with anyone.

In my media days, one of the consulting companies we worked with used the phrase:

> Fail Fast, Learn Fast, Fix Fast

I might re-jig that phrase to:

> Learn Fast, Implement Fast, Succeed Fast

In other words, learn what your customers want you to do better, make changes, and then be more successful on the back of the changes.

Learning and adapting to change I think is the new big business challenge, particularly for established businesses and for established business people, and for bigger businesses which have a culture of slow change - that is change that passes through meetings and committees and eventually happens. The danger is that by the time the change occurs customers have moved on and are seeking the next round of change. What did I say about the business challenge of 'Keeping up with customers'?

Learning shouldn't be regarded as a company thing. If people, particularly those in the customer facing areas, decide only to learn when 'forced' to, they will miss out and potentially get left behind in their sector. If you want to push on, be more successful, get promoted etc... don't wait for your company to organise a training day. Seize the initiative and do it yourself. There are enough resources - books like this plus articles, videos, podcasts, online courses etc...There has never been so much opportunity to learn, so don't waste it!

People do waste the opportunity to learn though.

I often think people get to a stage in their careers, particularly when they've done roughly the same sort of job for quite a while, where they think there is nothing more to learn.

Their knowledge, experience, and as they see it their expertise, reaches a point where in their eyes it is more than sufficient for them to be successful. They're the people who make a tidy living, have few ambitions, and without being unkind probably aim to make the most they can reward-wise, for the least effort.

As learning takes effort, it often evades their radar. All companies have these people. They reluctantly attend training or coaching sessions thinking they are a waste of time. Their mindset is 'I know my customers, I don't need to attend a session on Making the Most of Every Customer Interaction'.

During the build up to 44@60, the world was hit by the Covid pandemic when, as we know, all businesses and all types of business activity were affected in some way, shape or form.

Without doubt, the biggest transition or transformation for my business, was the move to delivering things on Zoom. I often joke that I had had a paid Zoom account for two years prior to the pandemic and had used it on probably two occasions.

What I did notice was that those people I mentioned above – the ones who had been doing the same sort of thing for quite a while – were the ones who struggled most to adapt to change, and as a consequence the need to learn new ways of doing business. Many of them resisted change on the grounds that this was a short-term disruption and that we would return to what they regarded as 'normal' at some point.

The learners though, and I count myself in that category, saw it very differently. For me I had no choice but to learn how to use Zoom, and I took the opportunity to make that transition to effectively a digital-only business, which in theory has increased my geographical reach massively.

Prior to the pandemic, I had carried out one podcast interview on Zoom, and now over the last 20 months, my guest list has expanded dramatically, with the vast majority being based in the US.

Delivering coaching and training programmes on Zoom has taught me that you have to learn a different way of delivering virtually, in comparison to in-person.

Apart from the technology, the people-interaction bit is different. The traditional in-person salespeople bemoaned that it was hard to build relationships on a virtual call. They're right, it is. But only if you are using the same techniques you use in-person.

In a podcast episode I recorded with David Roddick of kinzler.com.au he talked about how people have to recognise the different interaction skills needed when the meeting or pitch or presentation is virtual. David goes into significant depth explaining the way the brain works, and how it responds differently to people we meet in-person versus those on a virtual call. It's fascinating stuff.

Almost everyone in every company has had to learn, and will no doubt continue to learn, to do things differently. It must be very frustrating for organisations where their people kick back against change or simply pay lip service to it.

So my challenge to you as you read this section wearing your business hat is simply this:

What do you need to learn to do in the next 12 months that will ensure you keep up with your customers, stay ahead of your competition and demonstrate that you are always looking to do things better?

I have without doubt learned an awful lot about ultra running, but I am far from an expert, and my view is that I will continue to learn. That should be the view you take from a business perspective.

So one of the key business lessons from 44@60 is that you should never stop learning if you want to keep going forward and you aspire to continually be successful.

If you decide you know enough, others will undoubtedly catch you up and overtake you, and irrespective then of your experience and your believed expertise, you risk being left behind and losing your customers to others.

It's not about the way you want to do business with your customer, it's the way they want to do business with you. And if that means you need to change, then you would be foolish not to consider doing that.

If you have a good level of competence, particularly in the use of modern communication technology, you will be an asset, not just to your current employer and customers, but to your future ones as well.

'But Trevor I haven't got time to learn.'

Rubbish

If you're travelling, are you listening to the radio or music? Yes? Well then switch your listening to business podcasts. They are excellent learning tools.

Are you speaking to customers? Yes? In that case ask them questions which will enhance your learning:

'How do you do that?'
'What do you use for...?'
'Tell me how that works...'

Be curious when interacting with customers.

They will give you clues.

SECTION SUMMARY - TOP BUSINESS TIPS: KEEP ON LEARNING

- Get into the 'learning zone'

- Seize the initiative - don't wait for the company training day to learn new things

- Use your customers as a learning tool, they'll happy share what they know

- Avoid thinking 'everything will return to how it was pre-pandemic'. It won't

- 20 months in you are expected to be very proficient at running virtual meetings, delivering virtual sales pitches and presentations

- Use non-customer interactive time to learn. You can listen to podcasts whilst travelling, and videos when not driving

- Keep a list of all the things you need to learn how to do / use

- Don't confuse experience with learning. If you take the attitude 'I've been doing this for 20 years what more do I need to know?' you will get left behind

- Maybe not today but almost certainly tomorrow

- Learning is a legitimate business activity!

RUNNING DIARY; EARLY 2021

With the UK having experienced a further lockdown over the Christmas 2020 period, we started 2021 really not knowing what was going to happen.

What I did know was that the Classic Quarter was now scheduled for Saturday May 22nd, having originally been planned for Saturday June 6th.

The change was due to the arrival of what some would see as a rival event. The South West Traverse was to be run on exactly the same course on Sunday May 30th - the Sunday of the bank holiday weekend in the UK.

I'm not going to get into the politics of running events but there was seemingly some social media activity which was, in my view unfair on the organisers of the Classic Quarter. Comments from the 'new' event along the lines of 'finally a run this course deserves'.

In cases like this, organisers can't change the course - it's the South West Coast Path after all, which is pretty well fixed! What they can do is compete, if that's what they want to do, on the event support - food stations, runner communication channels, size of finisher's medal etc...

In the end, both events sold out, so many more runners enjoyed this breath-taking course, running either solo, in a relay of two or a relay of four.

And there is a business learning point here.

All businesses have competitors of some sort. You can ignore your competitors, learn from them, even work with them. Supermarkets compare prices, but they tend not to 'rubbish' each other. New businesses open all the time, existing businesses expand, so wherever you are and whatever business you're in, competition for customers will always be happening. My business advice is to focus on what you're good at, and aim to do even better the things you currently do better than others. That will help you stay ahead of the competition.

Running is, it seems, getting ever more popular - particularly ultra running - so as demand grows, inevitably more events are needed, which offers the opportunity for new event organisers to enter the market and existing ones to expand. And it can be quite lucrative if you get the model right and fill the places.

The upshot of all of this was that the Classic Quarter came forward two weeks to May 22nd, so as we started 2021 the event was less than five months away. Yikes!

One thing that did happen over the Christmas 2020 period was that I decided I was going to do some fundraising. This is detailed in the fundraising section, but 44@60 felt like such a big thing in my life that I needed to acknowledge it and raise some money for a great local cause, which as you will see in the fundraising section was the Music Therapy programme for the Children's Hospice South West.

There was no doubt that planning and launching the fundraising was a great incentive to train. It also removed, with the exception of serious injury or illness, my last opportunity to drop out! With fundraising money at stake, I had to do this, so I'd better launch into 2021 with some serious training.

And then bang - on January 4th, as we're all about to start running seriously after the Christmas / New Year period another lockdown was announced!

The upshot for runners was that all small-group runs were now off again, as we returned to exercising once a day on our own.

During the initial lockdown I had used a route planning system and some imagination to keep motivated. Time for this again.

I created a five mile 'run to work' route. I was very fortunate in that in the October before the pandemic I had built an office in my garden. How lucky was that? The upshot was that my travel to work route was out of my house, up three stone steps into my garden, across half a dozen path stones, and I was there. I've not measured or timed it, but it must take around ten seconds. The five mile route started at my front door and ended at my office door via various hills around Truro.

One of the ultra training techniques I read and learnt about is known as back-to-backs. Essentially running long on two successive days. Long, but not massively long, and running slightly further on the first day. The concept is that on day two your legs will have some fatigue in them from day one, so it's part of the conditioning to get used to running on tired legs, which is what will happen certainly in the second half of an ultra run.

I tried this for the first time in early January. On Saturday the 9th I did a 12 mile run, and on Sunday the 10th I did a fairly random run which got me to 10 miles. 22 miles in two days. It felt ok.

Another couple of long runs the following Saturdays - both 14-15 miles and around three hours on both occasions. I was told that training for an ultra is not so much about pace as 'time on feet' and around three hours is a good time to run for - especially at my age! That three hours also needs to be constant running - including all hills. 'Run up the hills in training, walk them during the ultra' was a lesson shared by both Andy Goundry and Edward Chapman.

Edward is an extraordinary runner. He only took up running in his 40s, and describes himself at that point as being an overweight accountant. He currently holds the record for the most finishes of the Kalahari seven-day desert event - 12 as this book goes to press.

It was during January that my daughter Bethany launched her own challenge, as part of her training for joining the RAF. Bethany had been offered a place in 2020 but unfortunately there was a delay in sourcing her medical record information, and there was also a delay in her pre-entry fitness test simply because all the gyms were closed. To help her, and give me an excuse for buying one, I bought a treadmill in the summer of 2020, so she could practice on that. The running part of her fitness test involved a timed 2.4km with a target of 13:23.

I've never been a big fan of treadmill running. It's the tedium of it that gets me. 30 minutes on a treadmill can see like an age, whereas when running 30 minutes on trails the time seems to fly by.

Bethany worked hard on her treadmill running, learning how to pace herself to hit that target time. Pacing over 2.4k to hit a target time on a treadmill is not easy, mainly because it always seems to take longer on the treadmill to get up to speed. So even if you work out the average pace needed to hit the target, which Bethany did, you do find yourself having to run the majority of the distance at above average pace to scale up for the inevitable slow start. The treadmill we have has a lap facility on it, so you can see where you on a 400m circuit. 2.4k being six laps meant one of the ways of hitting the goal was to set target times for the end of each lap. Watching where you are on each lap does break the treadmill tedium. The one upside of a treadmill time trial is the constant data you are seeing on screen, and it somehow feels easier to go all in on the last lap than it does outdoors. The surface is also at a constant elevation, not something you find when you run any distance where we live in Cornwall.

As with the preparation for any running, mixing up the surfaces and locations can be a great training advantage. To that end Bethany came up with the idea of doing a round-the-clock 5k challenge.

The challenge itself was starting a 5k on 24 consecutive days at a different hour of the 24-hour clock. Her work commitments meant a lot of planning as to which hour to do on what day. It was not going to be possible to do them in order.

I did a few with her, starting with the 4am one on Monday, January 25th. I'd never ever run at 4am before, so a first for me getting up about 3.45am to go for a run! And it was very icy as we ran around Truro - as well as quiet and still. Any insomniac curtain twitchers would have looked out on us and thought 'who are those nutters?'

The following day we did the 5am run. No ice this time just rain. After that I ran with Bethany at 10pm and 9pm - again times of the day I can't recall ever running at before. We also attempted to run different 'front door back to front door' courses. We followed this on the next two days with 7pm then 6am.

Clearly, lots of back-to-back 5k's are good, but ultimately I needed to do other stuff as part of my Classic Quarter training. As we entered February the clock was beginning to tick down. Only 16 weeks to go! Yikes!

The start of February also saw the launch of the fundraising campaign. Another stark reminder that this is for real! One piece of advice I was given was to avoid panicking as the weeks fell away. It would have been easy to start thinking - big gulp - in 16 weeks' time I'm running 44 miles - I'm never going to be ready!

As with most things, timing is a big part of success, and for me timing my training effort was key. Do too much too soon and you risk 'peaking' too early. Not enough and you risk trying to 'cram' training at the end. On reflection, and given that I completed the event, I'm thinking my training plan worked pretty well. On February 3rd I did a 10k 'time trail' using a largely off road route that we had used the previous summer. It was very wet and muddy but I was relatively pleased with 55½ minutes. Keeping up some speed work is a useful part of ultra training.

We finished Bethany's challenge with an 11pm run down a woodland trail, and then after a 25 minute stop back at the house we were out again at midnight for the 24th and final segment. I was very proud of her achievement, especially given the time of year. A number of people have since said that they would do something similar, although I've not heard of anyone who actually has. If you have, let me know! We could turn your round-the-clock adventure into an episode of the Running 44@60 podcast.

I did a 17 miler in mid February, and finished the month with 19 miles on the last Friday and then seven the next day. February's total was 102 miles which took me past 2,000 miles since the beginning of 2019.

March was the usual mix of various runs and routes, the longest being 20 miles on Mothering Sunday in the middle of the month. That was my longest run since the 2010 Eden Marathon.

7.
FUNDRAISING

It was over the Christmas holidays at the end of 2020 that I decided I did need to do some sort of fundraising.

Throughout the previous nine months, fundraising had become almost a national pastime, and hundreds indeed thousands of people had done some amazing things to raise money to help those who needed it during the pandemic.

Led by Captain Sir Tom Moore, who at the age of 99, decided to walk laps of his garden to raise money for the NHS. In the end he raised an incredible £33 million.

I was very wary therefore of doing my own fundraising, in case people were 'fundraised out', but I also knew that I would regret not having had a go at raising some money. And I also knew that it was likely that having a fundraising target would help motivate my training, and ultimately my run on the day.

By Christmas 2020 my daughter had finished her music degree from the Royal Welsh School of Music, in Cardiff and my son was in his third year as a medical student at Brighton. He also enjoyed music and both of them had without doubt benefited from the opportunity that music offered them when they were young at primary school.

I decided I wanted to raise money that created an opportunity for children to connect with music.

Over Christmas, and I can't remember what steered me in this particular direction, I became aware that the Children's Hospice South West ran a music therapy programme. The three of us had a good look at it and we collectively decided that the music therapy programme was what I should raise the money for. 2021 also happened to be the 30th anniversary of the Hospice.

In early January I contacted the Children's Hospice and, with the help of my daughter Bethany, we started to create a fundraising programme with a targeted launch date of February 1st, 2021.

Given all the fundraising that I mentioned above that had gone on in the previous nine to twelve months, I wanted to try and raise the money in a different way to the normal donation route.

First of all, I had to set a target, and in a sense this was the second part of the Big, Hairy, Audacious Goal. I decided I was going to raise £100 a mile, so £4,400. I told CHSW that I was going to get them £4,400, even if it meant underwriting it through a combination of myself and my business.

And it was the business sector that I was looking towards to raise the bulk of the money. During lockdown I had gained a lot of experience of running online business webinars, including three I ran for myself around the beginning of November which I offered for free, essentially to get some feedback and some practice.

I planned therefore three business masterclasses around the subjects of sales and presenting, and put together a schedule where all three would run twice starting on February 23rd, and then roughly every two weeks through to April 29th.

In keeping with the 44@60 theme my plan was to promote them as 60 minutes of action-packed tips and ideas with a fee of £44.

I was very confident, given my experience of the ones in November, that I would attract a lot of places.

That wasn't quite what happened.

It was a tough sell!

On the first one I had just two people. Thank you Stacey Halfyard and Greg Hobbs!

For the next eight weeks I spent a lot of time posting on LinkedIn, recording videos for LinkedIn, sending out emails, contacting former clients. It was a tough part of the whole thing, but every so often there was a big motivational spike when someone would book a place, or a company would ask me to deliver one of the masterclasses for their team.

The one that really made things motor was when I contacted the national sales director of a brewery based in Cornwall that I had worked with previously doing some sales and presentation training. I dropped him an email explaining what I was doing and to see whether he had a few people he might send on some of the masterclasses.

Within 30 minutes he replied to my email saying this was very good timing, and his first thought was that he would want me to deliver just for his team, with my session being part of a strategy plan to get the team ready to go back to business as the UK hospitality sector started to lift restrictions from mid-April onwards. Within the email he suggested there might be around 40 people and he would offer £1,000 to the fundraising.

That was the sort of email that made the time and effort promoting the masterclasses worthwhile. It gave me a huge lift. Thank you Martin Breading and St Austell Brewery.

In the appendix, there is a thank you list of all the companies and business individuals who supported the masterclasses.

There is also a list of all the individuals who donated to the fundraising.

I really enjoyed delivering the masterclasses.

'FUNDRAISING IS RELENTLESS, UPLIFTING AND MOTIVATIONAL'

They also created some great feedback for me through mechanisms like LinkedIn and Facebook.

One thing I did learn, which on reflection I had naïvely underestimated, was the reluctance seemingly for some businesses and individuals to invest in themselves.

Being based in Cornwall, and as such being relatively well known in the business community in Cornwall, was ironically going to be one of the big challenges, simply because businesses in Cornwall have, for around 20 years, got used to the idea of getting business help for free via various European funded schemes. (One of the ironies of the Brexit Vote was that Cornwall, which had benefited hugely from European money voted to leave Europe.)

The test of this was the correlation between those who were very happy in November to come on one of my webinars for free, versus then coming on a different paid-for webinar a few months later.

Those who came on all the free ones were on my webinar database, and I sent numerous emails to them explaining the benefits of investing £44, but few of them took it up, indeed hardly any. That was a disappointment. It was also another fundraising learning point - converting people from free to paid isn't easy - even though the fee was for charity. More on that in the revenue generating section.

So one of the big fundraising lessons for me was that, whilst I had what I thought was a great fundraising model, I had to a certain degree completely underestimated how difficult it would be to get people to actually pay for something that they had got so used to getting for free. On reflection, I had partly driven that outcome myself by offering those free webinars in November.

Overall, the big lesson I learnt about fundraising was that you have to continually and relentlessly keep pushing the fundraising at people. It also left me in total admiration of those people whose job is to fundraise, as well as those who are volunteer fundraisers. Hats off to all of you for doing what you do. There was no doubt that at certain times running 44 miles felt like the easy bit of the challenge!

Various people said to me, 'Oh yes Trevor, I will make a donation', but then they never did. I wasn't afraid to remind them, but even then, for many it never turned into a donation. I struggled to understand why those who said they would support me just didn't then do it straight away.

But there are two sides to most adventures and on the plus side there were some people who surprised me hugely with their generosity, when it came to individual donations.

Several people made some very chunky donations including £1/mile. A few people went further than that, and gave me much more including one of my old college friends who gave me £100, which I really didn't expect, and another who gave me £1/mile plus £1/year, so £104 in total. You know who you are, so thank you again for your tremendous generosity.

We did offer incentives! To try and attract individual donations we divided the 44 miles into 176 quarter-mile segments, and then give all supporters the chance to select one of the segments for every £10 they donated, with an incentive that when we did the random draw the winner would receive £75 (sponsored by my company) to spend on an eating-out experience for them and their family or friends.

We thought this would be a great idea and that everyone would buy into it and be keen to select their chosen numbers. In reality, hardly anyone picked up on it and in the early days we simply had to chase people and remind them to send us their chosen numbers.

We didn't keep that up for very long, but what we did do was as people donated we allocated the numbers for them. Due to the eventual success of the fundraising, we ended up with 216 segments, and that included excluding from the segment list close family members - we didn't actually tell them this - they're finding out now though!

I can confirm that we did use a random draw computer programme, and we did film the random draw to prove that we were doing it properly. The winner was the person who actually donated the largest amount. Of course it still meant their odds of winning were around 20 to 1, but in a sense it was nice that they were rewarded for their generosity.

On reflection, did the incentive make any difference? I'm not sure ultimately that it did but it was in keeping with our fundraising strategy of offering something in return. No doubt fundraising experts reading this will have their own views. Overall I would recommend when you are fundraising offering something in return if you can. I did where possible send a personal thank you message to each donor. Saying thank you, even if you do it by email, is easy to do and takes little time. It can have a disproportionate impact, particularly if those receiving the thank you are then motivated to tell others about your fundraising campaign.

It wasn't always possible to thank everyone because some people wanted to remain anonymous. There were also a couple of donations from people I wasn't sure who they were, and despite my trying to track them down they still remain unknown to me even though their names are listed as donors. If that's you and I didn't say thanks, I apologise for that. Thanks very much!

As we got towards the beginning of April, I knew that we were getting close to the target of £4,400.

So although I didn't change the target amount on fundraising platform JustGiving, I reset the target for myself to £100/year so £6,000.

I also knew at that stage that even though JustGiving was creeping towards £4,400, I had some business masterclass money which was agreed and had been invoiced but which had not yet shown on the fundraising tally.

We then amazingly went past £100/year and so the final target I set was £150/mile which was £6,600.

And we made it.

So what would I offer as a novice fundraiser as a summary of what I learnt about fundraising?

Here are my top five tips:

1 If you set an ambitious goal, that will not only motivate you, but it will help motivate your potential supporters, I think.

2 Constantly and relentlessly talk about your fundraising campaign – whenever I went on a training run, I wore some home-made 44@60 branding, and wore the Children's Hospice South-West running vest, so that whenever I met someone out running I would mention it.

3 Offer your supporters some value in return for their donation – in my case it was the business masterclass material or the chance to win the eating out £75 voucher.

4 Don't be afraid to remind people who said they would donate but haven't yet done so.

5 Where you can, thank all supporters personally as soon as possible after they have supported, and ask them to share the information about your fundraising with their friends, connections, colleagues...

The fundraising was relentless, but it was also very motivational, and I got a great thrill every time someone booked a place on a masterclass or made a donation via the JustGiving page.

Fundraising is a crowded market, but don't let that put you off. If you have a Big, Hairy, Audacious Goal challenge as I did, then fundraising can be motivational, it can help you get out and do that extra training run, and it gives you an excuse to shout about what you are doing, which in itself helps your motivation.

When I was actually doing the run, I used the fundraising to help keep me going, because every time my watch beeped to tell me I'd done another mile I realised I had raised another £150.

I was advised that, once the event is over, there will still be a flurry of donations, but for some reason that didn't happen for me, indeed of the £6,610, hardly any came in after the event, even though for the few days afterwards I did a lot of posting about what I had achieved.

And finally, finally, don't take things too personally in terms of who supported you and who didn't. In the two or three weeks after the event several people I met wanted to know about the run and congratulated me, but at the same time had not actually supported me. So don't let that bother you, just focus on the fact that you have raised a great amount and beaten your fundraising target, regardless of how that was achieved and who helped you achieve it.

Oh and there is something else.

What happens when someone who supported you does their own charity fundraiser - are you obliged to support them?

And what happens when those who didn't support you do their own fundraiser - do you not support them?

I've decided in these situations to ignore who supported me or who didn't, and imagine I hadn't done a fundraiser.

I then free up myself as I did previously to make my own call on supporting or not. Does that sound reasonable?

ATTRACTING BUSINESS REVENUES

So what are the business lessons from all the fundraising activity?

I think the first one is having a goal or target. I've met a lot of businesses, particularly one-person ones, and small companies, which don't have revenue goals.

If you don't have a goal, how do you know if you have been successful or even survived? You may have a great idea but if you can't convert that into enough revenue to make your business sustainable - well you know what happens next.

The fundraising goal I set felt like a Big, Hairy, Audacious Goal, and it was certainly a tough journey to achieve it. I think the same applies in business. It can be a tough journey to achieve your goals, one that you can easily end up giving up on or lowering the target.

One big lesson from the fundraising was to utilise and communicate with all contacts, which included current and previous customers as well as everyday connections. With previous customers, not only did the fundraising reconnect me with them, but for some subsequently it will have created future business down the line, something that may not have happened had I not been doing the fundraising.

Alex Goldfayn, author of 'Pick up the Phone and Sell' and 'Five Minute Selling' has been on my Better Presentations More Sales podcast a couple of times (episodes 127 and 182) and he shares a clear message - call (yes on the phone) your current customers, not in response to them but simply to check in with them. A call starts a conversation and that could well lead to additional business. And calling shows you care.

Emails or social messages don't have the same impact, simply because they are too easy to do.

Another big lesson was the fee for the masterclasses. It would have been easy after the first one which attracted just two people to have cut the fee to try and attract more numbers but on reflection I don't think that would have made a huge amount of difference. I think the real challenge was persuading people to pay for something in an online environment when they had got used to it being for free.

So although it was a tough sell, it also taught me that there is a market for paid webinars/masterclasses and that there is a value in them for the people attending. One of the challenges is to offer significantly better value than ones that are free and for buyers to recognise that value.

If it's free, is it really worth it?

Why is it free?

One of the lessons from the fundraising activity therefore, is not to undervalue what you offer, to back yourself to be worth that value, and to ensure that when you do get the opportunity to deliver for your customer, you exceed their expectations.

Make sure you acknowledge everyone who hires you in, buys your product, buys your service, by thanking them as best you can, certainly personally, and ideally, if they are happy for you to do so, publicly as well.

That thank you is all part of the value of the investment they made in you.

How many times have you had a personalised shout out from someone on LinkedIn whose free webinar you attended?

Never I suspect!

So how can fundraising lessons be linked to sales activity?

To generate revenue for your business, you need to create sales of your products or services.

And in business 'sales' is one of those words that we are not usually that keen on. We prefer to have people just give us the money for our product or service without having a conversation around a 'sale'.

Here are some tips from the fundraising that will, I believe, help you generate revenue for your business, through sales of your product or service, in the same way people bought a masterclass or gave a donation.

'DON'T UNDERESTIMATE THE VALUE TO OTHERS OF YOUR PRODUCT/ SERVICE'

Firstly, make it easy for people to understand your offering. You may think that your product or service is very easy to understand in terms of what it does, how it works, how it is delivered, how it is priced etc., but that may not be the experience of your customers and in particular your potential customers. So have a good look at what you offer and be really challenging in the way you market your offering.

If potential customers don't understand the offering when they see it, on your website, or in your social media activity, or your marketing activity generally, or indeed when they meet you at an event when you explain it to them, then they aren't going to buy.

In my opinion, especially for small businesses, lots of business opportunities go to waste because the potential customer doesn't understand what the offering is, and in particular the benefits of it to them if they buy.

Secondly, make it easy for people to subsequently buy your product or service. You may think that it's really easy to buy whatever it is you offer. Again, is that what your customers and potential customers think?

When was the last time you tried to buy something from your own company?

Try it and see what happens – you might be surprised by just how many barriers there are, that you have inadvertently put in place that actually stop people from buying your product or service.

You need to identify and then do your best to remove those barriers to sales. It's hard enough getting on the radar of potential customers, as it was getting on the radar of potential supporters and masterclass buyers when it came to the fundraising, so don't then make it even harder to convert those people into customers.

Thirdly, as with the fundraising, keep a track of the data. You may well have a target for revenue generation for your business, but if you don't track how you are doing against that target, then it's almost pointless having a target in the first place.

Don't wait for your annual meeting with your accountant to find out how you're doing in terms of revenue generation and what type of revenue generation.

I essentially had three revenue streams for the fundraising: Individual donors via JustGiving, business individuals and businesses who booked places on the specified masterclasses, and businesses who hired me to deliver one of the masterclass themes exclusively for themselves and their team.

It was this final stream, that in the beginning I hadn't really recognised as a source of fundraising, but in the end it produced a significant amount – indeed around 40% of the total raised came from these individual company masterclasses.

So in hindsight if I was to do this again. I would probably focus on delivering masterclasses for companies. rather than trying to sell individual places as I did.

In business our offerings pivot, often on the back of customer actions. In this case it was companies asking for their own Masterclass that opened up this fundraising stream. As Better Presentations More Sales podcast guest Michael Reddington said in episode 172 'customers give us clues' - clues as to what they want us to do or offer.

I would probably have run the three masterclasses once only for the individuals, and given myself a bit more time to sell the places on them. I wouldn't have changed the price though.

As I did with the fundraising, you need to be prepared to recognise that your sales/revenue target is likely to fluctuate, ideally upwards but realistically it could be downwards.

So here's a question for you:

How many revenue streams exist in your business through your product or service offering, that didn't exist three years ago?

And as a secondary question, going forward into your next business planning year, how many revenue streams will be in your business plan that aren't currently either in your current plan, or make a very small contribution?

In section five we talked about shouting or marketing. If you are going to generate revenues, as I set out to generate fundraising, you have to do lots of shouting or marketing, and not just occasionally. It needs to be relentless!

Some of that shouting needs to be aimed at sector of clients we often overlook from a marketing point of view – our existing or former customers.
Of all those people who hired me to deliver business masterclasses for their team, virtually every one of them had been a previous client.

Customers or clients stop using us for various reasons – everything from a project finishing to a training programme being delivered right through, to falling out with one of our team or indeed ourselves. One of the biggest reasons in the B2B sector for customers leaving is that they no longer feel appreciated. Don't let that happen to your customers!

Whatever reason your former client left you, don't forget that at some point they hired you, which means at some point they trusted you to deliver your service or product for them, and presumably they liked the idea of you doing that, which is why they chose you instead of your competitor.

And when we look at revenue generation in business, we can easily overlook the future opportunity that previous clients can create.

Usually this is because we are reluctant to have conversations with previous clients in case they say things about us which we don't fully want to hear. You might be surprised how many previous clients are ready to rekindle that buying relationship with you. Sometimes you just need to ask.

Even if they left you because there was a clash of people, often those people that the clashes were with have moved on, either from your company or from the company you did business with.

So from a revenue generation point of view, get back on the previous client's radar.

Reconnect with them. There are many ways to do that from simply phoning them up, to interacting with them on something like LinkedIn, sending them some useful advice and information, going to a networking event which you think they will attend.

And if I was to offer some revenue generation and fundraising advice, I would say the best thing you can do is to simply be proactive.

In business we are very good at being reactive, responding when things happen rather than making them happen.

Indeed we are more comfortable being reactive, and we're good at it because we get lots of practice handling incoming calls or enquiries, responding to messages, dealing with complaints etc...

But if you want to make a real difference to your revenue generation then you need to be proactive, and that doesn't necessarily mean lots of cold calling or other old-fashioned ways of trying to attract business, it can simply mean attending a virtual networking event, delivering a preprepared, well practised elevator pitch, making the best comment on a social media post placed by a prospective client, talking to your existing customers about extra products and services you offer that they don't currently purchase, growing the profile of your business and yourself etc....

It is very easy to hope that revenue generation just happens.

But as with fundraising, if you take that approach then you are in a sense 'hoping for the best'.

On the other hand, if you take a proactive approach to revenue generation, then not only are you likely to be more successful, but that success will have a knock-on effect in terms of momentum within your business for yourself and your team.

So make things happen!

I finished the fundraising section by talking about those who asked me about how the fundraising went but who actually hadn't supported it.

You will get that in business.

People who are ideal customers, who show great interest in your product or service but then don't buy it.

You know the ones. If you've ever sold a house, they are the ones who turn up for a viewing armed with a tape measure, a sketch pad, and interesting questions. They say lots of complimentary things. They leave and you think they are a cert for a second viewing and probably an offer.

The agent never hears from them again!

And that happens in business.

During the fundraising I discovered that on LinkedIn you can create an 'event' and send a direct invitation to any of your connections.

Once I discovered this, I created an 'event' for each masterclass. You can add all the details and make it very clear if it is paid or free.

You then literally scroll through your connections and tick the ones to send the invite to. Now this did work for me. I'm sure a few places were sold on the back of this.

However I also experienced what I'll call 'false hope'.

When you receive such an invite - and if you're on Linked In you've probably had one - you can tick a box to say you are attending.

When I first used this I got very excited when around 12 people ticked the box to say they were 'attending'. To actually attend they had to follow the booking link and pay for their place upfront by card or PayPal.

I kept cross referencing who said they were 'attending' with who had booked and paid for a place, naively thinking there would be a 100% match!

I was so wrong!

The majority who said they 'attending' weren't booking. I decided to contact them. I dropped them an individual LinkedIn message saying how pleased I was that they had said they were attending but reminding them - I think subtly - that they hadn't actually completed the booking. And then three things happened:

The odd person did book - fantastic - and if you were one of them, thank you very much.

Others made all sorts of excuses as to why they could no longer attend - I think only one had the balls to say that they hadn't realised it was a paid event and they couldn't afford it - fair enough - although it was only £44 not £440 and it was all going to the Children's Hospice South West.

The rest ignored my message - bear in mind these were all first connections not random unknowns.

But as with those who promise support and then don't go through with it, you have to avoid getting too hung up on this or indeed taking it personally.

I did carry on using the 'event' posting for all the masterclasses. And it did produce some paid places.

And yes, I did keep sending out reminders to those who said they were attending and didn't!

Those got far less as the series moved on. Perhaps word spreads not to say you were attending and then not book a place because if you did, I'd be on to you!

The bigger picture is the overall goal. If you hit that, does it matter sometimes how ultimately you got there?

And then there's luck.

The magical business ingredient we all hope for.

I was fortunate some years ago to be part of a leadership programme run by DMGT, the parent company of Northcliffe Media. One evening during the middle of the programme our dinner guest was the group vice-chairman David Dutton. Mr

Dutton was one of, if not the first, business person in the UK, to recognise that we needed pizza.

He also recognised the importance of the location of pizza outlets. This was in the 1960s. Roll on to the 2000s, and over dinner he asks myself and the other 11 delegates from across the world a simple question. What are the seven most important factors that make a business successful?

I recall that between us we got the first six fairly quickly including be determined, be smart but not too smart, make the best of what you've got, test your ideas, the importance of humour in business.

However as hard as we tried the seventh one eluded us.

It was 'luck'.

Mr Dutton explained how important luck was to business success. The caveat though was that luck was something you could influence.

Work hard, be proactive, be relentless in your pursuit of success and hey ho, from time to time you'll get lucky.

In business there will be times when we feel like some sales were 'lucky'.

So get out there and make your own luck!

SECTION SUMMARY - TOP BUSINESS TIPS: REVENUE GENERATION

- Make it easy for customers to understand your offer and buy it

- Don't think you are 'selling', think you are 'helping'

- Position yourself as a customer asset - someone who becomes invaluable to them

- Be enthusiastic but not overwhelming!

- Build your connections - personalise all connection invites

- Respond quickly to all enquiries

- Phone, don't email

- Ask big questions

- Be relentless with your marketing

- Send out proposals in a written and video format

- Surprise and delight your customers - a simple thank you card works wonders

- Listen, don't talk! Shutting up is a key sales skill!

RUNNING DIARY; APRIL 2021>

At that conference back in February 2019, prior to listening to Jim Lawless, I had decided that I was going to run a third marathon when I reached 60, to go with the two that I done - Amsterdam in 2005 and Eden in 2010.

However, a few weeks before my 60th birthday and inspired by the fact that in 2020 my daughter Bethany had run a half marathon for the first time on her birthday, I decided that it would be good for my training and also to get that third marathon ticked off, if I ran a marathon on my actual 60th birthday, which turned out to be on Good Friday. It was during a time when numerous virtual races were taking place.

I'd simply do my own virtual race with me as the only competitor. If I got round, I'd be taking home various prizes - first overall, first in age category, course record etc...

This would be a marathon based on a course that started and finished at my house. I live in Truro in Cornwall, so it was always going to quite hilly. And in complete contrast to the 44@60 campaign, I decided that I would tell absolutely nobody about this, with the exception of my two children, Bethany who was still in Cornwall having finished her degree and waiting for her next career move, and Jim who was back from university in Brighton for the Easter holidays.

I planned the course using an online mapping system (Mapometer). Bethany wanted to run the last 10k with me, which was going to be back and forth along an old tram line (the Newham trail), half a mile from the house. Jim was suffering from a bit of a niggly knee injury, so decided to focus on taking responsibility for meeting me at roughly 14 miles, to change my water bottles over and replenish any gels.

Trying to ensure my run reached 26.2 miles as I got back to the house was a bit tricky, even with sophisticated planning software. The planning including some part-course recces, and the odd flirtation up and down a road just to get the distance right.

April 2nd arrived and all was looking good including the weather. The plan was that I would start at 8am. On a Friday, Bethany had been doing some voluntary dog walking for an organisation called the Cinnamon Trust, and had been going off around mid-morning to walk an ageing cocker spaniel for a couple who needed help with that task. So she explained that she was going to go and do that earlier than normal, so she had plenty of time to get back, get changed and then meet me for the last six miles.

I thought nothing of that at all, as it seemed very logical to me as she headed off at 7.45am. So Jim was the 'starter' as I set off I set at 8am with my hydration vest loaded up with food and drink for the next five hours.

The first leg of the route took me down into Truro. Around three quarters of a mile in I would go through an underpass into the Garras Wharf car park. From there I would run out to the village of Malpas and back, reaching around six miles before heading out towards Idless and Shortlanesend. This first six miles was carefully selected as it would be relatively flat, so an opportunity to get into the flow of the run. It also followed the river, so lots of things to observe and distract me from the distance ahead.

As I started to come out of the underpass I could hear some people chattering. It was quite early in the morning on a bank holiday, so I thought it seemed a bit odd.

Surprise! As I emerged into the car park, I felt suddenly very overwhelmed because there were four of my running buddies and Bethany taking a bit of film on her phone.

They simply said to me, 'we couldn't let you do this on your own Trevor'.

Now usually in something like a marathon if you're going to get overwhelmed in an emotional way, then it's probably when you get to the last mile or so and you know that you are going to achieve your goal. This was the opposite. I had absolutely no inclination that these friends of mine were going to join me on the run, so to see them was a complete surprise.

And to put this into context, I had been very lucky with the timing, because it was only on the Monday of that week that the government had announced that we were able to go back to running in groups of up to 6 people.

Completely unbeknown to me, Bethany had meticulously organised what turned out to be a total of 15 support runners to join and leave at various points on the course. I then realised why she had left so early. What a ruse that was!

And it confirmed why, in the last couple of weeks before the run, she had been so interested in the tweaks I had been making to the course in order to get the distance right. Little did I know she was masterminding a series of support runner changes. As I write this it makes me realise just what an operation Bethany undertook to make this happen, and to get the timings right, based on my likely pace, and thus arrival at the various points where the support group changed. It made me feel like Eliud Kipchoge when he was running the sub two-hour marathon in Venice, as like me his support group continually changed during the run.

The first group took me through the first six miles in about an hour, which was a good one minute a mile quicker than if I'd been running on my own. A good start to my aim of doing a sub five hour run, knowing that in the middle part of the course there were going to be a few tough and long hill climbs.

One of the things I had planned to keep me motivated throughout the birthday marathon was to every so often record snippets for an episode of my Running 44@60 podcast, but with so much going on around me, I found myself chatting along pretty much all the way around with the support runners. I think I only managed to record three snippets of the podcast, so episode 48 would ultimately be quite a brief one!

It was an extraordinary day and I did manage to finish in 4:56. I hadn't properly checked beforehand, but I thought my Eden marathon time was around 4:53, so with a couple of miles to go I did wonder whether I could push on and actually beat that time, but that was going to always prove difficult and I was more than happy to settle for 4:56.

A big thanks to everyone who took part - you all get a mention in the appendix. Special thanks to Bethany for supreme organisation, especially for setting things up in such a way that I had no inkling whatsoever as to what was going on until I emerged from that subway. She may not have realised it at the time, but Bethany had clearly passed the audition to be crew manager for the big run!

The support illustrated just what a great community runners are. I've been involved in many sports over the years, usually team ones, but running is different. The camaraderie is just fantastic.

I ended up doing 120 miles in April, which was only two short of my personal best for a single month. That had been the previous April, which of course was the first full month of the pandemic lockdown, when we were all adapting and trying to take full advantage of the 'rule' that we could only exercise once a day, and indeed exercise was one of the few reasons you were allowed to leave your house. Seems somewhat surreal reflecting on April 2020 as I write this, 18 months later.

With the birthday marathon completed, I was now just seven weeks away from the Endurancelife Classic Quarter.

Those 120 miles in April were spread over 11 runs. I did four runs of between three and seven miles before the next long run on the 16th, two weeks after the marathon.

The 16 miles was on a route that started from my house, and then as much as possible was off road and included taking me through some woods in the St Clements area of Truro. Essentially an out and back route with a bit of a loop at the turning point so it didn't feel as though I'd run eight miles in one direction and then turned around and come back.

The next day I went down to the National Trust property at Trelissick and ran about 12 miles around the woodland trails and paths. 28 miles over the two days. The longest combined back-to-back runs so far.

I used these runs to practice eating. Remember one of my advisors had told me that the Classic Quarter was as much about eating as running, so it was time to practice eating, particularly what some runners describe as 'real' food (non-real food being gels, energy bars etc.)

Somewhere, I read or heard about hot cross buns as a great ultra run food source. I planned therefore to try these alongside my own flapjack. I selected Sainsbury's apple and cinnamon hot cross buns, and lathered them with crunchy peanut butter, then cut them into quarters. The key I discovered is to eat them very slowly, nibbling at the edges so you make a quarter of a hot cross bun last several minutes.

There are two good reasons for using this eating technique: firstly eating gives you something to do whilst running. And anything you do whilst running is a great distraction from the running. This proved particularly useful as the hours passed during the run itself. In the distraction stakes, I supplemented eating with podcast recording, and salt tablet chewing (on the hour). Having a set 'eating / activity' schedule really did help the time go by. As detailed later, during the Classic Quarter itself I ate every three miles.

The second reason for eating slowly is that you're more likely to be able to eat. More on that in the eating and drinking section.

My home-made flapjack contained various things such as chopped dates, sultanas, peanut butter, flaxseed and maca powder, as well as the usual flapjack ingredients. The recipe is detailed in the appendix section.

The key point here is that practising eating in training is a crucial part of your ultra run success.

Those back-to-back longish runs were a great opportunity to practice eating. And don't wait until your last couple of training runs. You need time to know what works for you. I'm lucky in that I've always been a good eater. I am largely vegan and my food choices worked for me. Choose yours and give them a proper go - which includes eating early - for me that was from three miles in. It's the same with drinks and gels. Use these long runs to sort out what works for you.

These last few weeks of training were now bringing the whole two-and-a-bit year plan together.

Also in the last few weeks of training, and especially over the long runs, I had to get my head round not trying to do them too quickly, but to run at a pace not far off the pace I would be aiming for in the event itself. I do think that sometimes as runners we get too obsessed with times and pace and all that sort of stuff, whereas my real plan for the back-to-back runs was just to get used to running for a longish time over a two-day period, and to see how my legs would react on the second day having done 16 miles on day one.

I know I'm in danger of thinking, as I share my experiences, that I'm already some sort of ultra running expert. With just one ultra run under my belt clearly that is not the case. However I do think I became an expert ultra runner 'student'. In other words, someone who soaked up all the ideas, advice and tips from the experts and then applied it. If you're reading this as a build up to your first ultra, then I suggest you take the same approach.

If you want to succeed you need to keep learning!

Whether that's ultra running, running a business, or life in general.

The next part of training was more course recceing. Some runners feel the need to run the course several times. They like to think they know every inch of the route.

I was a bit casual in my approach for two reasons. Firstly, I'm hopeless at remembering courses. If a friend enters a race and asks me if I've done it and I say yes, they'll say 'what's the course like?' and I'll say 'I can't remember'. Others will recall races and say, 'remember how the course went ....and then it ... before it.....'. I look at them blankly and say, 'No I don't!'

That for me even applies to parkrun. I've not checked the precise numbers, but I suspect I've run the Trelissick parkrun 70+ times, and I've set it up at least 20 times. Yet when I'm pushing on in the last mile, I still struggle to remember all the curves and twists!

Secondly whilst I wanted to get a feel for the course, I wanted some element of surprise as well. Ideally not nasty surprises - more like stunning views I hadn't seen before, interesting monuments etc...

In 2020, I had run as part of the relay with Andy Williams the first 25 miles or so, which took me to the end of Marazion. I knew the second half of the course would be harder. I broke it down into three parts:

Part 1 - The rest of the road section from Marazion to the end of Mousehole. Hang on I hear some of you saying isn't the Classic Quarter run entirely on the South West Coast Path? What's this talk of road sections? To clarify. From the beginning of Marazion to the end of Mousehole there is no coastal path in terms of a narrow series of footpaths, trails, routes through fields/ across beaches. The terrain doesn't exist on the coastal edge so 'the path' through that eight mile section is a combination of pavements and road.

Back to my recce plan.

Part 2 of the second half is the section from the end of Mousehole to the Minack Theatre. This is described as the most 'technical' section. I was thinking, like you maybe are right now, - what do they mean by 'technical'. What can be 'technical' about running along a coastal path? The same path thousands of people of all shapes and sizes and ages successfully negotiate each year.

I now know that the word 'technical', when applied to ultra running, refers to sections where you won't be running. You will be scrambling, or more likely treading carefully, as you clamber over or around the odd large rock or work your way up or down a series of narrow steps. In most cases you won't need specialist mountaineering gear! That section is around eight miles.

The final part, the final five miles, is across open country from the Minack Theatre to the finish at Land's End. I purposefully decided not to recce that bit. The final cut off was at the Minack. So, if I made that I could enjoy the final five miles going as fast or as slow as I liked, or more likely as fast as I was capable. I decided that not knowing the last section would keep me motivated. I did though decide to recce the Mousehole to Minack section with its 'technical' bits.

On the Wednesday after my back-to-backs my daughter Bethany drove me to the point on the course where the road section finishes and runners re-join the 'normal' coastal path. This would also be the point during the run where I would change back into my off-road shoes. The recce therefore was useful to Bethany, as my crew manager, to know where the changeover point was, how to get there (you approach it down a back lane) and where to park (on the side of the lane).

I noticed that on their website the organisers had a picture of a pair of runners scrambling over what looks like a couple of big rocks. My plan during the recce was to find them and see if they were as daunting as they looked.

Turned out they were just after leaving the cove at Lamorna. They weren't easy to get over, but they weren't as daunting as the photograph made out, and it was only one big rock not a whole series of them as I had imagined.

There was one bit on the section which, as I approached it, did feel quite daunting, especially because I'm not brilliant with heights these days. I'm very happy to shin up a ladder at the side of a house, but I think it's the looking down over the cliff edge that I'm not great with!

Just before getting to Lamorna the path goes around the sea side of a rocky outcrop. It did feel like you were close to the edge, and I was gently tip toeing my way around. It must have been only for about 20 yards. It was one of those moments when you think about those crazy ultra runners who do this part of the coast path in the dark at the end of January in the 100 mile Arc of Attrition. I'm never doing that. You read that here first!

In the actual run I was with another a runner, and as I was leading I ran round it without a second thought.

So it was really useful to run that section and get a feel for it. I think it took me about two hours 20 minutes, but of course I was running on fresh legs rather than ones that would already have done 32 miles, as would be the case on the day. My thinking was that if I could do that section on the day in around three hours then I should be fine for getting to the cut-off point at the Minack within the time allowed.

My final course recce was the following Tuesday (April 27th) when I went back down to the course and ran the road section from Marazion cemetery to the end of Mousehole. I had been told by various people that this section was six to seven miles. I'm not sure what measurement tools they used, because it is actually about eight miles.

I parked in the middle of the section at Penzance station. I turned right and ran as far as the old Penlee lifeboat station which is about a mile from the end of Mousehole. I turned around and ran back past the station to Marazion, 14 miles in total of road running. I'm not sure if this was really needed but it did give me a feel for the road section, and gave me a run on the road, for a change.

I think a lot of people would not practice running the road section, but for me I just wanted to check how it flowed, and how it worked through Penzance in particular, because even though it is the official coastal path it clearly doesn't feel like that because you are running largely on the pavement.

I'm now less than four weeks away, so just one more of the back-to-back runs to do and I'm done.

April 30th and May 1st - a Friday and Saturday three weeks before the event, and my last back-to-back runs. I largely replicate the runs from two weeks previously. The 16 mile out-and-back along the river trails, and then on the Saturday almost 13 miles at Trelissick.

It felt strange when I finished the Trelissick run. I knew that was my final longish run and that in three weeks' time it would be the real thing. All that training was now coming into the taper stage. More on that in the next running section.

I had now completed 346 runs and 2,266 miles since the beginning of 2019. The fundraising was just about complete - the business masterclasses were finished - the overall target had been hit. It was now ideally three weeks of ticking over, staying injury free, following the eating plans I had been given and being ready and focused when the big day arrived.

8.

EATING AND DRINKING

When I started on this adventure, course specialist Andy Goundry told me (in episode three of the Running 44@60 podcast) that the Classic Quarter was an eating competition as much as a running one!

He was right!

If you hear people talking about running a marathon, they may mention 'hitting the wall', the point at around 20 miles where suddenly you feel devoid of energy and all you want to do is stop.

Some years ago, a cricket playing friend of mine, Kevin Bosustow, was fortunate enough to get a place in the London marathon. He trained hard for this first marathon and was all set. I remember being at a christening that day in Cornwall, and trying to discreetly follow Kevin on my phone using the London Marathon race number tracking app.

At around 23 miles, he disappeared off the app. I was in rural Cornwall, in the days before superfast broadband, so I just assumed that it was a technical hitch.

Unfortunately for Kevin that wasn't the case. At that 23 mile point, he collapsed on the course, with dehydration. He ended up in hospital with his legs packed with ice. He made a full recovery but the moment had passed and he never attempted a marathon again.

You can imagine how difficult that must have been, knowing that you are essentially a parkrun away from finishing the London marathon, and next thing you know you've stopped and your race is done.

It had been a warm but overcast day, and as most experienced runners know, conditions like that can catch you out because you think you don't need as much liquid in those conditions as you would if it was very sunny. The bottom line was that the temperature on the day was not vastly different to what it might have been on a sunny day. It was just that the overcast conditions convinced Kevin he didn't need to drink as much as he should have done. Staying hydrated is so important when long distance running.

'AN ULTRA IS AN EATING COMPETITION AS MUCH AS A RUNNING ONE'

It might well have been Andy Goundry who also said to me that when you're running an ultra you need to eat before you feel hungry and you need to drink before you feel thirsty.

That is top advice for anyone running any sort of distance beyond a half marathon, but certainly for a marathon and definitely for an ultramarathon. You don't want to risk not finishing not because you haven't trained enough but simply because on the day you didn't drink or eat enough.

Here are the key lessons that I learnt about eating and drinking:

Firstly you need to practice eating and drinking. I've met several runners who practice running parts of the course of the ultramarathon they are going to do, but not many of them practised eating and drinking.

Think about eating and drinking early in your training. That gives you the opportunity to discover what works for you. Better to establish that a drink or gel or proper food item doesn't sit well in your stomach during training than during the race.

It does feel a bit odd taking flapjack and hot cross buns on a 10 mile training run but you'll get used to it. If on race day you're going to eat and drink every three miles, then eat and drink three times on a 10 mile training run.

Secondly, you need to have something that you can carry your food and drink in and get used to wearing. My go-to piece of kit for this is a Ultimate Direction hydration vest, which has lots of pockets as well as the opportunity to carry drink flasks and a separate drinks bladder.

Prior to acquiring the hydration vest I had used various belts with water bottles that you carry round your waist with some pockets for gels etc.

The hydration vest was the first thing I purchased after I made my announcement about running the Classic Quarter. Just coming out of my local running shop with a hydration vest and the bits that go with it elevated me, in my own mind, to being on the way to becoming an ultra runner.

Indeed every time I went out on a training run and took the hydration vest with me I felt more and more like a proper runner.

Acquiring the hydration vest was one of the game-changing moments, as far as I was concerned, because I quickly realised that it was ultimately much more comfortable to carry the drinks and foods and gels in the vest rather around my waist.

So if you're reading this and you are planning that long run, either a marathon or ultramarathon, then I would definitely recommend a hydration vest.

Get used to wearing it and drinking and eating from it, and ignore any of your running friends who say things like 'Trevor you're only doing 6 miles, why are you wearing your hydration vest?' (Was that you Jim Spencer?)

One other top tip with regard to the hydration vest is that the bottles which are non-rigid may not come with what are known as straws. These are tubes around 3 inches long, which stick out from the flask, and I found made it much easier to drink from.

I also bought a second set of drinks flasks, which proved really useful on the run because it meant that when I got to my crew meeting point and needed to replenish my drinks, they simply took from me the empty bottle, took off the straw top, replaced it on the bottle they had already filled and handed it back to me. This was a very efficient way of topping up my drinks bottles.

So what to eat?

I was given lots of different tips on what to eat by various experienced ultra runners including the following:

Flapjack
Mini Cheddars
Mini malt loaf
Watermelon
Hot cross buns
Cherry tomatoes

Sandwiches
Crisps and Peanuts

I'm sure this list would grow if you talked to ultra runners you know, all of whom will have their favourites.

And then there are gels, small packets of gooey stuff packed full of energy-enhancing ingredients. Love or hate them it's probably a good idea to train yourself to take them. There is choice galore, so I can only mention the brand I use. Torq gels come in a variety of enticing flavours such as banoffee pie, apple crumble, rhubarb and custard, strawberry yoghurt, lemon drizzle, Bakewell tart, raspberry ripple etc. Sound delicious, don't they?

Here are the foods I used during the Classic Quarter:

Homemade flapjack
Homemade banana bread
Apple & cinnamon hot cross buns - cut in half and laden with crunchy peanut butter then cut into quarters.
Mini Cheddars, which are good for salt intake

My crew also had Jaffa cakes, mini malt loaves, watermelon and baby tomatoes.

I also took with me a selection of the gels.

What I found during the run was that I was able to eat the flapjack and the hot cross buns quite easily in the first half, but then in the second half I just really didn't fancy any more flapjack or hot cross bun, and I largely ate things like watermelon and tomatoes washed down with flat Coke.

As far as drinks go, I had one 500ml flask with water in it, and the other one with the Torq electrolyte drink which for me was the pink grapefruit flavour. There are numerous flavours of electrolyte drink to choose from so have a go at one or two and settle then on the one you prefer. Plain water is good for washing down food and gels.

I was fortunate to get some great advice from nutrition experts. Daz Stephens of Kinetic Energy Nutrition provided me with lots of eating advice, and ultra runner Anna Pascoe of Make Me A Plan, created a seven-day plan for me which included eating six times a day in the final build-up to the run. Anna has won two 24-hour races, so she knows what she's talking about.

I regard myself as almost 100% vegan, and therefore my plan revolved around that. I'm not going to detail everything I ate in those last few days, but it did include carbo loading in the two to three days before the event.

This included pancakes and pasta, featuring a perfectly timed pancake recipe from the May 2021 edition of Runners World!

Anna's six stage daily eating plan involved three main meals and three snacks in between.

The main meals weren't huge, and the snacks included rice cakes, fruit and chocolate. Essentially the whole idea is to get used to eating at regular, shorter intervals, because that's exactly what will be happening during the run.

I made my own smoothies, which I used during the training and the final build-up. My go-to recipe for the smoothies was a bit haphazard and included whatever I could lay my hands on including:

Spinach, mint from the garden, frozen summer fruits, kiwifruit, beetroot juice, kale, grapefruit juice, ginger and then some water if it looks as though it's going to be too thick!

My go-to food for breakfast prior to a run of any length is porridge based. On the day of the Classic Quarter this meant having porridge at around 5:30am. I believe it is absolutely vital that you have a big breakfast, regardless of the time you need to eat it and regardless of whether you are feeling hungry.

My porridge breakfast is a combination of equal amounts of jumbo porridge oats, coconut milk and water, slowly cooked for about 20 minutes. I'll add a dash or two if maple syrup and a sliced banana and have it with a cup of strong green tea.

I also took a small flask of green tea and a banana to have at the start whilst I was waiting for my start time to come along.

So what about eating during the run itself?

I've listed out the things that I took with me, but as far as I was concerned the key strategy was to eat before I was hungry and drink before I was thirsty.

Given that I had consumed a significant porridge breakfast around 90 minutes before I actually started, I could probably have easily run for two or three hours without the need for any food.

But all the advice I was given was not to do that but to eat early.

I broke the Classic Quarter into 15 segments of essentially three miles each. At each three mile marker I would eat, drink and record a minute or two for my podcast.

This breaking down of the run into the 15 segments not only helped me come to terms with just how far I was actually running, but it also ensured that I never felt as though I was running out of energy, during the whole run.

So at three miles, which was around 45 minutes in, I tucked into the flapjack and whatever else I fancied that I was carrying, and I made sure that every three miles I repeated this eating process.

I wasn't taking on large amounts, probably one quarter of a hot cross bun and one cube of the flapjack, but it was enough to ensure that I was effectively and continually topping up my energy resources.

For those who did not finish, but technically weren't injured, did they eat and drink sufficiently? and sufficiently early? or did they not eat drink enough and simply hit the 'Wall'? I imagine if you do hit the wall in an ultramarathon, then that is not great news and makes it hard, maybe impossible, to carry on.

Hitting the wall with 10k to go in a marathon must be bad enough, but hitting the wall in an ultra, with maybe 10 or 20 miles to go. That's tough.

The other top tip I can share, with regard to eating on the run, is to eat slowly.

If you put a quarter of a hot cross bun in front of me right now I could probably demolish it one bite in a few seconds. On the run I was nibbling at the hot cross bun quarter so that it lasted me several minutes.

And anything you can do on the run that distracts you for even a few minutes is always going to be of benefit. One of the challenges of ultra running, I discovered, is to ensure you are distracted enough not to keep thinking about how far you still have to go! You want that next mile beep on your watch to come round what feels like really quickly!

f you are using a crew, you need to give them a reasonable idea as to what you will want them to replenish each time you meet them.

With my crew, we went through a detailed plan so that they knew how many gels I would need at each point, whether I needed my drink bottles completely replenishing, and which foods I wanted to take on board and carry with me for the next section.

It is also useful if the crew have extra bottles of water and your electrolyte drink which you can just drink from when you meet them, as an added top up. This also works for things like watermelon and cherry tomatoes which are difficult to carry safely, so I tucked into them whenever I met the crew.

Indeed, those runners around me also tucked into the food and drink my crew were carrying, because I had given them enough to last a week!

As mentioned already, there is a road section, between Marazion Cemetery and the end of Mousehole.

Watching one of Loyd Purvis's excellent Run4Adventure running videos on YouTube I noticed that in the 2020 version of the event he had met some of his running friends on the Penzance promenade and had handed ice lollies to them. So I thought 'well if it's good enough for his team it's certainly good enough for me', so that's what I did.

And because that part of the course is all tarmac it was a great to have that ice lolly. I understand some of the runners who were just behind me enjoyed them as well, as my crew handed out lollies to them. If that was you, I hope you enjoyed the lolly!

My 'lolly crew' were my son Jim and his girlfriend Cass. I hadn't met Cass before, so I imagine a fairly unusual meeting of your boyfriend's Dad for the first time - handing him an ice lolly 30 miles into a run, and whilst holding onto a great motivational hardboard sign they had made. That sign is now on the wall in my house.

Not all runners have a crew, and instead will rely on organisers' aid stations for top ups of both food and drink. In that case it's important that you carry with you food that you want to eat that you know won't be available to you at the aid stations.

I didn't actually eat anything at any of the aid stations, but I did drink plenty of flat Coke.

Several people who came on the Running 44@60 podcast talked about flat Coke including Colin Bathe. Now I don't mind the odd Pepsi Max on a hot day, but I wouldn't say that I was a regular Coca-Cola drinker. However, following that advice I supplied my team with a large bottle of full fat Coca-Cola which we took the top off overnight to ensure it went flat.

The first time I drank any of it was at the Marazion Cemetery crew checkpoint, which was my second meeting with the crew, at 24 miles in.

When I arrived at that second checkpoint, I knew that I was in need of a bit of restoration, and I was amazed how well the watermelon and the flat coke worked for me.

I did think that the flat coke, which inevitably would also start to feel a bit warmed up, would actually be a bit ghastly, but in reality it wasn't and I think the sweetness of it was the big benefit.

One of the things I was advised to do was to brief the crew to say, whenever they saw me, how great I was looking - even if I wasn't!

And apparently at that 24 mile marker I *wasn't* looking great, but interestingly a mile further on, the crew saw me again as they had gone to a car park to treat themselves to an ice cream, and they said that I was looking remarkably different. So I can only put that down to a combination of the 10 minute rest I had at that crew point, and the flat Coke and watermelon!

The one thing I did consistently take on board during the whole run were gels and salt tablets.

I don't know how many it was in total but I suspect probably eight or nine gels over the 44 miles, at relatively consistent intervals. Certainly in the second half of the run having those enticing flavours such as Banoffee Pie and Apple Crumble make it much easier to take them on board.

I think it was Loyd Purvis who advised me to take a salt tablet every hour, which I did, although I forgot completely at the end of the first hour, so the first one I took was actually around one hour 45 minutes.

After that I religiously took them on the hour, and I had no sense that I was getting cramp or anything like that at all during the whole run.

An ultra run is realistically only achievable if you have a robust eating and drinking plan.

One that you practice during training. It is easy to underestimate the impact the food and drink has.

So eat before you're hungry and drink before you're thirsty.

NUTRITION IN BUSINESS

So what can we learn from eating and drinking as part of the planning and on the day activity for running an ultramarathon, when we are wearing our everyday business hat?

Maybe we should reflect firstly on why we do all that eating and drinking when we are running an ultramarathon.

It seems that there is only one reason for it, and that is to have enough energy in the tank to complete the run.

And yes it probably does sound a bit like a picnic when you read through all the various things that I ate before and during the run.

So in business how often do we think about what we are eating and drinking during our everyday business activity?

Do we give it any thought at all?

I work with a lot of business people, and I have noticed over the years some fairly big changes to our business attitude to eating and drinking. These changes have probably been connected to the consumption of alcohol, and what was known back in the day as the 'business lunch'.

All of us are in such a hurry these days that the 'business lunch' has fallen away, because we no longer think we have time for it. The business lunch at one point was regarded as a key business tool. You entertained your client, or prospective client, for an hour or so, during which you had a great opportunity to find ways of doing more business or gaining a new client. People buy from people and the one-to-one business lunch enables that to happen.

My media career started in 1983, and it was in the 1980s and the early 90s when the culture of work boozing was at its height.

I remember being on a trainee managers course in 1986 and spending a day with the very experienced team at our national sales office in London.

The day was designed for myself and my colleague to shadow one of the experienced national sales team, a guy called Bob, who was probably in his 60s at that point.

We went to one of the big London agencies that spent a lot of money in regional press, and I remember sitting in on what we assumed was a big sales negotiation session.

At what felt like a crucial moment, the negotiation was interrupted by the media director of the agency who insisted on steering Bob away from the meeting to his extravagantly large office, to view a painting he had recently acquired.

My colleague and I weren't sure what to do next, so when Bob returned we just tagged along, as everybody departed for the local boozer, where the beer started flowing and everyone played darts.

In the taxi with Bob and my colleague on the way back to our office, I remember Bob looking at us both, and saying something along the lines of: 'You young whippersnappers are wondering what on earth happened today, aren't you?'

'Well this is what happened. In the pub we concluded one of the biggest deals the regional press has ever seen. And the point I want to make to you, as you start your career, is to remember that often it's more about the doors you can open and the people you know, than your ability to be a hotshot negotiator.'

You don't need to run an ultramarathon to run your business, or manage your team, or be good at your job, so why be concerned about eating and drinking?

'DON'T UNDERESTIMATE THE POWER OF GOOD NUTRITION IN BUSINESS'

So here's a thought:

What difference do you think it could make to your overall business performance if you adopted an eating and drinking strategy based around maintaining your energy levels, and therefore your sharpness, throughout the whole of the working day?

Maybe I should ask this question in a slightly different way – how many of you reading this book, who work in the business sector, have experienced an afternoon slump? Or indeed any period in the day when you are simply not able to maintain your 'A Game' because you are feeling tired or lacking in energy?

In today's world, nutrition coaches, such as the previously mentioned Daz Stephens, work with businesses to help them help their people to be as sharp and as energised as possible, throughout the whole of the working day.

If eating and drinking is so important to top sportspeople who have on-hand dieticians and nutritionists, then why shouldn't it be important to the business sector?

The nearest I've witnessed to something in action that addresses this is when I was fortunate in the mid-2000s to spend some time at the Ashridge Business School. I remember during the conference breaks, the nibbles were largely fruit and nuts, or as they described them 'brain food'.

Usually at a business event or conference, during the breaks you are going to be tempted with delicious and hugely moreish biscuits, cakes etc... and then you experience the sugar lift followed by the sugar decline.

Personally, I've always found that eating at an event where I'm sitting and listening, does make me feel drowsy. Is it the food, or the event agenda / speakers?

So could eating and drinking in business actually position itself as a differentiation tool?

We might think that the business lunch has had its day, but I don't agree with that, because I do think that if you are able to meet a prospective client for lunch, then you have their undivided attention for probably 60 to 90 minutes, so therefore what a glorious opportunity that is.

Someone once asked me how I would suggest they ensured the entire client lunch isn't spent on the 'small talk' - I suggested to use the order point as a trigger. As soon as the waiter has taken your order, switch to business talk!

The other big tip that I took away from that time in Ashridge was the simple statement that in business you have to 'look after yourself', and that could mean eating healthily and properly during the working day, rather than grabbing a meal deal to eat at your desk.

I think in business we can learn an awful lot from eating and drinking, in both preparation and execution of an ultramarathon.

Like with the running though, it is a question of attitude.

Firstly, we need to be convinced that our business eating and drinking habits can make a difference to our success.

And then if we do believe that is the case, then we need to do something about them, and not just some token gestures such as of baskets of fruit arriving every few days.

There has to be a proper joined up approach, where the company offers advice to its people on nutrition, as well as drinking including coffee, tea, fizzy drinks, water etc.

If you are a top sportsperson you would take this very seriously.

So if you regard yourself as a top business person, or someone who aspires to be a top business person, the question you have to ask yourself is ‘are you taking your business eating and drinking seriously?’

SECTION SUMMARY - TOP BUSINESS TIPS: NUTRITION

- Eat regularly to maintain your energy levels
- Drink plenty of water to stay hydrated
- Recognise the benefits workplace nutrition can bring to business
- Avoid most workplace vending machines
- Bringing in your own lunch means no 'nipping out' for a pasty or meal deal
- The business lunch is a great opportunity to do business
- You don't have to eat all the biscuits on offer during an events break!
- If you are running a business seek advice from a nutrition expert
- Invest in them to do a nutrition audit and create a plan
- Have them share their ideas with your people, including the benefits to them as individuals
- Take nutrition in business seriously

RUNNING DIARY; TIME TO TAPER

Including the birthday marathon, two back-to-back runs and a couple of course recces, April's mileage came in at 120. Only two miles short of my highest ever monthly mileage.

May 1st was the 13 mile part two of the final back-to-back run. Three weeks to go, and time to taper.

Tapering can be a tricky time for runners. You've got so used to running regularly and running long, if you are preparing for a marathon or ultramarathon, and now you have to rein yourself in and reduce your running significantly. Tapering is a time to rest and build your energy stores.

The hardest part of tapering, I've discovered for many runners, is overcoming the fear that during tapering they will lose their fitness, stamina, running sharpness etc... It's why many find this part of the training hard to accomplish. They end up doing more running than they should, during the tapering period.

I think I'm pretty good at tapering. For me it was three weeks to relax, tick over and reflect on what I had achieved so far: 346 runs and almost 2,300 miles since the beginning of January 2019. It is also a chance to create and check your kit list, to map the route, and in my case work with my crew on the crew plan.

I ran four times in those last three weeks. All runs between four and eight miles. I had planned no road runs, but my mate Andy Williams, who I ran the relay of two with in 2020 and who was now in for the full 44, wanted to do an eight mile steady road run.

I agreed.

I do remember it being quite warm and sweating an awful lot as we pounded the back roads around Truro.

My main concern was avoiding picking up a silly injury - tweaking a calf muscle or accidentally stepping off the pavement or anything ridiculous like that.

Fortunately I avoided all such hazards. Indeed, I had been hugely lucky to avoid injuries throughout the entire two years of training. The only injury of sorts my running diary notes was in the summer of 2020 when I was doing some gentle running followed by a 'time trial' along the first mile of the Trelissick parkrun course. I felt a top of thigh tweak so rested for a week.

My final run was on May 15th, the Saturday before the event. Four miles, gently around Trelissick, with my daughter Bethany. The film crew that followed me on the day were there for the final run to record my thoughts at that point.

During the fundraising campaign I had been contacted by Simon Bert and his wife Anna, who run a photography business. Simon was keen to move into video photography and offered to film parts of my run as his contribution to my fundraising activity.

The meet up with Anna and Simon at Trelissick before the start of the final steady training run enabled them to do a bit of filming, including me explaining some of the kit I was taking. We also went through the event with Bethany, my crew manager, so they would know the best places to film me and also roughly when I would be at those places.

This final training run took the number of runs since the start of 2019 to 350, and the total mileage since then to 2,292.

The final week build up included a sports massage for my legs from Lee Wheston, checking all my kits, re-checking the course route, and having a Zoom call with my crew to check the plans with them.

I re-watched the Run4Adventure video on YouTube of the 2020 Classic Quarter, I checked Google Earth in case I missed any woods I needed to go through.

I was also eating six times a day following Anna Pascoe's plans.

One thing I did notice was that I started to think I was carrying a small hamstring tweak, that I had a minor sore throat, that I had some toothache coming on. All nonsense of course, but your mind and body can start to test you in those final few days when largely all you've got to do is think about the run.

On Friday morning I just did my usual commute from my office to the kitchen to make a cup of tea, a massive hike of about 20 steps, when out of nowhere my right foot felt painful. What's going on? This can't be happening! That evening I went over to the crew house in Mawnan Smith, and the foot was still hurting as I went up the stairs to dump my bags. I told no one and assumed by morning it would be gone. It was.

Having 'weighed in' at just over 190lbs at the beginning of 2019 I was around 174lbs before the last couple of days of carbo loading. I felt primed and ready.

Bethany's boyfriend Craig arrived around 9pm from Lincolnshire. Jim and his girlfriend Cass weren't expected to arrive until 11pm. Too late for me! I was in bed by 9pm and asleep shortly after that. Fortunately I've always been a good sleeper. The alarm was set for 5am.

9.
THE BIG DAY ARRIVES

MAY 22ND 2021

I woke at 5am as planned, having had some good sleep. My slow cooked porridge with maple syrup and banana was consumed about 5:30 and my ex-wife Annabel drove me down to Lizard Point to the start.

We arrived in good time at the National Trust car park which was only a few minutes' walk from the start line.

My official start time was 7:08:30. Because of COVID, all runners had individual start times. I thought this was a good idea and for a run like this, much better than a mass start. A mass start means everyone wanting the loo at the same time, having to arrive on the start line 10-15 minutes before the actual start, and then jostling for position, and inevitably on a course like this queuing at the first stile or series of steps. And when that queuing happens you look at your watch and think 'this is too slow', and you find yourself thinking you need to speed up even though you've only been going less than a mile and have the best part of 44 to go. Individual start times is so much more civilised.

And yes, I can hear you say 'but doesn't individual starts take away the element of a 'race' - person v person competing against each other' etc... I agree to an extent it does, but only realistically in that first dash off the start line. And let's face it, no matter how big or small the field of runners, only four or five, or maybe six at the most have a chance of winning.

The start times were 'graded' so that those who had a chance of winning all went off first. And at 20 second intervals it means you have to gain less than half a second per mile over 44 miles to overtake the person who started in front of you.

So for events with narrow starts or likely traffic jams early on, let's go for individual starts, or if necessary as a compromise, small group starts.

When we arrived at the car park it was raining, so on with the rain jacket and waterproof cap and gloves. One visit to the loo, a last slurp of green tea and bite of a banana, and I'm ready to go. No turning back now!

I make my way to the start. Simon Burt the photographer does a short interview with me, and I introduce myself to the Endurancelife start team. They had kindly adhered to my request to give me number 60 for the event, which was on one side of my shorts with a homemade 44@60 on the other side, which included the Children's Hospice South West logo. I was advised to wear my number on my shorts rather than on my shirt as it makes it more visible at checkpoints when you are wearing a hydration vest or rain-jacket, and if you do wear it on your shirt and then decide for whatever reason to change your shirt during the run you don't have to unpin your number and pin it to the new shirt. I assumed few, if any, runners would be changing their shorts during the run.

I'm a couple of minutes early but they point a clock-like machine at me and I'm away.

It was quite a moment. 815 days since the bravado at the business event of 'I'm going to do the Classic Quarter in 2021' and the stuff that followed. People often say that the hardest thing about running generally is getting out the front door and starting the run. And for a big well-planned event like this run, one of the biggest challenges can be simply getting to the start line - that is avoiding injuries, illnesses etc... that ultimately prevent many runners actually starting the event.

Incidentally I'm writing the second draft of this section on a Saturday night in an AirBnB in Newport. The night before the Newport marathon. The event I had planned for April 2020 as part of my training for the Classic Quarter relay of two that summer. Writing this is helping me get in the 'zone' for tomorrow!

Back to May 22nd 2021 and I was on the start line and then a few seconds later I've been 'zapped' by the timing device, and I was on my way. Those first few steps in the rain and I'm trying not to think of the hours of running I had ahead of me, trying not to get over excited that I was on my way, trying not to think I already needed a pee.

During my research into long distance running, it became clear that the challenge is as much mental as it is physical. Sure, running 44 miles will be physically tough, but it won't be constant running. The physical part gets broken up by the terrain changes. There'll be plenty of walking up hills. There'll be running on paths, across fields, on roads, through woods, over rocks etc... There'll be the crew meet ups.

In a sense the physical part is taken care of by all those varying environments. Mentally though, the conditions don't necessarily help. I learnt that the key to mental success was focusing on small segments, thinking ahead only to the next landmark, creating distractions, and remaining positive by smiling a lot, chatting to anyone on the route, and trying to enjoy my big day out.

So here was my cunning plan: break the route down into three mile segments. Not just as they happened but plotting them on my course map, which is now framed up in my house and has all the three mile segment post it notes stuck to it.

The three mile segment plan had lots of things going on to distract me. At the end of each three miles I would:

Record a snippet for my podcast, eat and drink. This involved doing stuff and every time you do stuff in a long run you focus on that and not the running. The running is just happening. It's subconscious running. Sure, you don't want to trip over or take the wrong route, so you're not completely switched off but you're away from the 'moment' as you focus on trying to extract from a pocket on your hydration vest a quarter of a rather squashed hot cross bun that is neither hot or looks anything like a bun.

'THIS IS IT - AFTER 815 DAYS OF PLANNING, I'M ON THE START LINE'

The extraction process also involved none of the other quarters escaping from the bag they are in, or worst of all the whole bag escaping. That did happen during one of my recce runs. I went for a piece of hot cross bun and found an empty pocket. Somehow, when I had eaten the previous bit, the whole bag had fallen out without me realising. I always moan about people leaving rubbish on the coastal path and then it was my turn! I can just imagine someone out for a walk coming across a plastic bag with a cut up hot cross bun inside and chuntering on about tourists dropping litter!

Each podcast snippet required taking my phone out of a pocket and pressing record on the voice memo app. I had a cable running up my vest from the pocket to a small microphone attached to the top of my running vest. I had also invested in what was marketed as the best outdoor microphone muffler! Something that looks like a rabbit's fluffy tail which goes over the small mic head, and allegedly keeps out the noise of the buffeting wind and / or rain. Largely that did work ok.

So podcast snippet recording, then something to eat - not the gels but the hot cross buns, the flapjack, the banana bread, sometimes a combination of two or even three of them.

I would eat slowly, very slowly. It passes the time. Once the last crumbs had been swallowed, I would have a sip of water to wash it all down. This eating and running at three miles also ensured I didn't fall into the trap of waiting until I was hungry before eating and waiting until I was thirsty before drinking. Small regular top ups. The same applies to marathon running. Take stuff on board as soon on the run as it becomes available. Don't wait until you think you need it.

At the end of each three mile section I 'started' a new 'parkrun'. Fifteen three mile segments means 15 parkruns. Try it. During the Newport marathon there were lots of home-made signs out on the course with messages such as 'Only 7.5 parkruns to go'. We talked about breaking big business goals down into small segments elsewhere, but whatever you are doing breaking something down into units you are familiar with and confident about will help with the mental side of the task.

I named each of the 15 parkrun segments after a parkrun I had tackled, starting with the furthest from home, Guernsey, and working my way back.

Running at around 13-14 minutes per mile means the miles won't slip by in a flash, but by the time I'd done all my three mile actions, the best part of another mile had passed.

You can do something similar in training. From ten miles onwards I would have a bite to eat every half mile, and a sip of drink every mile, alternating between water and isotonic. My training runs never exceeded 20 miles so having that routine for the second half of a long training run definitely helped pass the time.

The other routines were gels - roughly every 90 minutes - and salt tablets - one on the hour, every hour.

Just before six miles, my friends Suzie and Martin Hearn appeared at the Marconi Monument, armed with a banana which I ate half of. Meeting people like that *en route* always gives you a lift.

There was a beach crossing at nine miles to the first check point, then another beach crossing at Loe Bar, which was 12 miles in. By now the rain jacket was off and in my hydration vest and there was just the right amount of sunshine for long distance running.

The next landmark was Praa Sands, at around 18 miles. It was also my first planned meet up with my crew.

There was a slight difference here, because the previous year the route had gone across the beach, but this year the course had changed, so I came into a car park which I assumed was the car park the crew were in.

I couldn't find them. Logic told me that given the preparation they had undertaken as crew, that they would be in the right place - we had mapped it out using what3words. It must be me that was wrong. I was 'rescued' by someone who obviously realised that I was struggling to work out where I was. They told me there was another car park about 50 yards along the road.

Ok. So off I went. 50 yards down the road there was Anna Burt the photography lady.

She said my crew were in position in the next car park. Exactly where we had planned! It was great to see Bethany and Craig. We changed the water bottle, added an extra gel, I ate half a banana and went to the public loo, although not really sure I needed it. And then I'm off.

At 20 miles I had my one and only mental wobble. My watch beeped to tell me 20 miles was gone. That was great, but it hit me that I still had 24 miles to go. I'd only run beyond 20 miles four times in my life before today - the Amsterdam Marathon in 2005, the Eden Marathon in 2010, the 'birthday' marathon in April and last year's 25.7 miles when I ran the first 'half' of this event.

The latter proved very useful at this stage, as I had run this part of the course before and the memory of that helped me get over the 'mental' moment and head on towards the next crew stop at Marazion Cemetery, 24 miles in.

That would be the end of my eighth three mile section but in terms of a bigger breakdown, I had divided the run into four 'quarters' from a mental point of view. I felt it was important in terms of motivation not to have four equal time or distance quarters. My quarters were as follows:

Q1 - Start to Marazion Cemetery - 24 miles
Q2 - Marazion Cemetery to the end of Mousehole - the road section - eight miles
Q3 - Re-joining of coastal path to Minack Theatre - eight miles
Q4 - Minack to finish - just less than five miles

I arrived at the Cemetery. Time for a sit down. A proper crew stop! I changed into road shoes so a chance to re-grease my toes (top tip for avoiding blisters), change my socks, take on some sun cream - although I forgot the back of my knees which did get sunburnt.

On such a long run, it's good to take this type of break. I just sat on a piece of granite and took on watermelon for the first time, and drank some flat Coke. As mentioned in the previous section, part of the crew brief was to tell me I was looking good even if I wasn't! Later they told me I wasn't looking great at this stop.

The 'hard surface' stage takes you through Marazion, through Penzance via the promenade and to the end of the famous fishing village of Mousehole.

Before Penzance the walk/cycle path was in parts being repaired. During my recce run, I had reached a cafe with some steps down into the beach. On the day I got as far as the cafe and asked the staff if this was the route. They said yes. I went down onto the beach and trundled along for around three quarters of a mile. It was hard going. And I didn't need to do it. I had inadvertently been given duff info. The run route had been diverted around the path repair not via the beach but the road! I had missed the diversion sign.

As we ran into Penzance, I stopped at the run aid station manned by Edward Chapman. Ed has been on the Running 44@60 podcast twice, firstly early on to offer long distance running advice, and particularly for this run. Second time around he talked about his adventures in the Kalahari Desert Classic. It's a seven-day carry-all-your-gear event. Ed holds the record for most completions. Tune in if that event interests you. I downed some flat coke and headed for the Penzance promenade. By now I'm about 30 miles in.

Seeing 30 miles appear on my watch was a first time experience. I'd never run 30 miles before, so that was some moment. In my head, I also hadn't got that far to go - a mere 14 and a bit miles!

Along the promenade I had the ice lolly from Jim and Cass, my crew at that point. They had ice lollies as well as motivational sign made from a piece of hardboard. The sign is now on the wall in my house, as well as the banner Bethany made.

Just before I reached the ice lolly point, Simon Burt shot some video. I asked everyone to cheer as I ran towards Simon, telling them he was there to film me. Made me feel like a celebrity! No doubt the people I asked to cheer were intrigued to know who I was! Or maybe not!

Penzance turns into Newlyn, and the waterside turns into a harbour full of fishing boats. In Newlyn I came across another runner who had stopped. I asked if he was ok. He was struggling so I suggested we run together to Mousehole. My new running buddy Sam was from Newquay. He was mid 20's and this was a big first for him in running terms.

We ran to the start of Mousehole where Sam's girlfriend was meeting him. This was his opportunity to drop out and it appeared that was his plan. I carried on and was surprised when my parkrunning mate Mike Gray appeared out of nowhere. He had ridden his motorbike down to Mousehole for lunch. He knew the event was on and knew I was in it, but it was a sheer coincidence that he appeared just as I was running through. He jogged along with me for a while.

Mike departed and Sam re-appeared. He had decided to carry on and asked if we could run together over the last 13 miles or so. 'Absolutely', I said. Running with Sam undoubtably helped me through those last miles, as we took turns to lead and simply chatted about all sorts of stuff. Sam was very knowledgeable and would point out landmarks and give detailed accounts of them.

The hill out of Mousehole is tough! At the top were Bethany and Craig, ready for a full-on crew stop, which included changing back into trail shoes, taking on board watermelon, baby tomatoes and flat Coke.

We now faced the toughest part of the route. The eight miles to the Minack Theatre via Lamorna Cove.

Just before you get to Lamorna Cove, there is a bit of a rocky outcrop which takes you pretty close to the edge, and has a great view down into the sea quite a way below. I had edged my way around this in the recce run. I was now leading Sam at this point, so I took on the role of run leader and never gave the terrain or drop a second thought. We skipped around it and headed down into the Cove and the penultimate checkpoint at 33 miles. We were ahead of the cut off by about 40 minutes. We stocked up and set off for the Minack.

Other runners arrived at the checkpoint as we were leaving. The first ones we had seen in a while. Always good for personal morale if you're leaving a checkpoint as others arrive.

The section to the Minack felt much longer than when I recced it. Maybe because I had an extra 30 miles in my legs on the day! I thought I had mapped the section out quite well in my head, but on the day, every ascent was the one I was thinking would show the Minack at its top. It didn't!

Goodness knows how many climbs and steps this route entails. Probably best not to know.

Eventually we did see the Minack Theatre.

Crews weren't allowed on site at the Minack because there was a performance going on.

The crew meeting place was where the path from the car park down to Porthcurno beach crosses the coast path. The stop was brief. I was confident I had 20 minutes in hand, but it would be pretty disastrous to hang around with the crew and miss the cut off by a minute!

A last top up of drinks bottles, some final watermelon, the pick-up of a spare emergency gel and I'm up some tough steps at the side of the Minack (not the ones at the back of the stage which is where the footpath actually goes). At the top of the steps, it's a short run to the checkpoint.

Everyone here seems in a buoyant mood. Perfect as a tonic. Just under five miles to go. For the first time a chance to slightly relax.

For me, this point in any long run is a golden moment. In a marathon or half marathon, it's the two-miles-to-go marker. You know at that stage, bar a serious injury or mishap, you are going to make it. I felt like that at the Minack.

No longer could I be timed out. If I had to walk, or even crawl to the finish, I would get there. I was actually feeling pretty good. Running with someone else, in this case Sam from Newquay, was a big plus. Our conversations about nothing in particular kept us going.

At the Minack I pledged to be back in 2022. But not as a runner. As a volunteer at the Minack aid station! Whilst we do our best to thank the volunteers when out on the run, it's worth saying here and now what a fabulous job they do.

Marshaling or manning an aid station is not just about offering directions or handing out drinks and Jaffa cakes, it's the words of encouragement that make the real difference. So to every volunteer on the 2021 Classic Quarter route, a very big 'Thank you marshal'!

During the Newport Marathon in October 2021, the 'extra milers' as the volunteers were called, excelled themselves when it came to encouragement. If you are a volunteer, please keep shouting!

If you're a runner who hasn't volunteered - even at a parkrun - do so. You'll find it hugely rewarding. Writing his has prompted me to contact Endurancelife and remind them of my volunteer offer for 2022.

As we headed off towards Land's End I remember one of the podcast guests advising me not to look too far ahead too often. They said that you will see Land's End often, but it will feel like it never gets any closer.

Whoever that was, you were right! (Apologies if it was you and I've forgotten that.)

Sam and I ploughed on, and every time we came to a steep downhill followed by yet another arduous uphill, we were convinced it was the last hill, and that at the top we would see Land's End. Not just see it, but be within touching distance.

Emerging from the top of yet another big climb we could see it alright. But it wasn't yet within touching distance, as we could also see between us and the finish yet another big down and up!

In fact I think we did six more down and ups from the moment I thought it was the last one. But hey ho, why rush to the end now. We need to soak this up. Live in the moment. As I write this, I'm visualising progress through those last couple of miles. My GPS was closing in on 44 miles when we saw the famous event sign: 'One Mile to Go!'

Finally we emerged from another 'down into the valley, climb up the hill the other side' section and there it was. Land's End. And no more valleys or hills between us and the finish.

With 500 yards to go there was a slight incline, and the path was becoming more road like. I suggested to Sam that we emerge from the top of that final incline in running mode and that we cross the line together. Not quite Dick Beardsley and Inge Simonsen crossing the line together at the end of the first London marathon in 1981, but our version of it.

Because of COVID, the organisers had encouraged crowds not to gather at the finish. We knew though that my crew, Sam's girlfriend, and my photographers would be there.

We lapped up the cheering and crossed the line. That was it. Job done. 30 seconds over 13 hours. I didn't really care about the time, although I won't miss the opportunity to tell you all that I was third in my age category. And before you run off and check, there were only three finishers in my age category. There were though five starters.

My crew of six were there with Bethany's banner. We had photos taken. I gave an interview to Simon Burt, the videographer. I collected my medal and finisher's running shirt.

It was 8pm, but the ice cream I promised myself tasted delicious! Was I feeling totally exhausted? Not really. I do think your body adapts. I was out there for 13 hours but not constantly running. As advised, I walked up all the hills. I stopped at aid stations and crew meeting points.

We got back to the crew house in Mawnan Smith at 9.30pm. Dinner was chilli and rice. I ate some but I wasn't able to eat that much. I thought I would eat for England.

I guess your body needs to time to re-adjust after 13 hours of movement and being fed hot cross bus, flapjack and gels etc.

I did have a pre-eat soak in the bath for 15 minutes with some bath salts, that turned the water a sand colour. I can highly recommend the bath salts.

If training runs finished at my house I would soak my legs in a cold bath using the formula of one minute per mile. The first few seconds are tough, but the water warms up, or feels like it warms up very quickly.

By 11.30 the crew party was in full swing, but I was ready for bed.

And then I couldn't sleep.

My legs were very tired but my brain was buzzing.

I had done it.

I kept thinking about the journey from the impetuous announcement at the business conference, the training and finally the run itself.

By 8am the next morning we were in the sea at Maenporth.

YOUR BIG BUSINESS DAY

Your big business day could be a key presentation to a client, speaking at an event, pitching your business plan to investors, the first day of taking over another company, starting a new role, moving into new premises, the launch of a new product or service.

The exact nature of your big business day will be specific to your situation, but whatever it is, try to enjoy that day, and try to remember as much about it as possible, as I did with the run.

No doubt you will be feeling a little bit trepidatious, a few nerves will be jangling as you try and contain your excitement against the balance of feeling scared!

But, like with the run, if you've done the preparation and the planning and some practice, you should be confident that whatever it is you are hoping to achieve will happen.

During my business career, our big business day of the year was when we presented our next year's business plan to our national Board of Directors.

Whilst we spent a long time preparing the plan, the key goal was simple: get approval for a plan that matched the expectations of the directors in terms of revenue and profit generation, whilst feeling confident that we could achieve it.

It was a big game. And bonuses were at stake.

The key to a successful business plan delivery, and gaining acceptance for it, is understanding the rules of the game and playing to them.

If you are too cautious you are asked to be more optimistic, and if you are too optimistic you are asked to be more cautious.

The skill was understanding where the parameters of overcautious and overoptimistic were and then delivering something in between.

Naturally, on the board there would be those who were looking for anomalies in the plan, numbers that didn't add up, contradictions between the narrative and the numbers etc... so you had to be very alert to what was being asked and how you are going to answer it.

Whatever *your* big business day involves, investing in preparation and planning will help you achieve success.

'ENJOY YOUR BIG DAY BUT FOLLOW UP TO KEEP THE MOMENTUM GOING'

Whenever I work with people who deliver key presentations, one thing I discover when I ask them about previous key presentations is that more often than not they underprepared. That usually translates into them not focusing enough on the outcome they wanted to achieve. In hindsight they left too much to chance, and then were prepared to blame a lack of success on bad luck.

When I was running the Classic Quarter, bad luck would have been slipping on a rock or something similar, that resulted in an injury that made it impossible to carry on.

Bad luck would not have been running out of energy, getting too dehydrated to carry on, getting sunburnt, wearing the wrong shoes etc... Any of these events could have halted my run. All of them were avoidable if the planning was right, which I like to think it was.

The nearest I actually came to an injury was stubbing my toes three or four times, simply through carelessness, as I was running along. Those mistakes though were not big enough to affect my overall performance.

You *will* make small mistakes on your big business day; the trick is to not allow them to become big mistakes and therefore risk you not achieving your goal.

The Gary Player quote – 'the more I practice the luckier I get' has been used exhaustively but nevertheless remains true – I may have mentioned it once or twice already.

So it will be very rare when you can genuinely blame bad luck if your big business day doesn't work out.

Here's what you can learn from my run, in terms of preparation for your big business day:

Create a list of all the things you need to remember to do, and all the things you need to have with you on the day, plus try and identify some back up contingencies just in case you need them.

For example if I'm working with someone on a key presentation I always ask them to have a Plan B in case say the projector stops working and they have to do the presentation without slides. This rarely happens but you don't want 'surprises' of this nature on the day to throw you.

Detail the timings of the day so you know exactly what you need to be doing at what time.

Don't skip breakfast, because the last thing you want to do on your big business day is to start to flag early on and run out of energy.

Make sure you have a good breakfast and then, during the day, keep topping up your energy and hydration levels.

On any run, you keep moving, whether that's walking up the hills or running on the flats. On your big business day, you need to keep moving, because if you stop for even 30 minutes you may lose your momentum.

And when it's over?

Take a few minutes to reflect on what happened.

What worked?

What didn't work?

If you could have the day all over again, what would you do differently?

Did you achieve your desired outcome?

What do you need to do next?

With the run, it was in a sense a one-off. When it was finished it was over. The next day I didn't have to think about doing it again.

Your business big day will almost certainly be the start of something, rather than the end.

That great presentation wins you a new client; now you have to deliver on the new client's expectations - the reasons why they said 'yes' to you.

The inspiring presentation to your staff or team went down a storm; but you then have to ensure all the parts of it happen.

You gained some significant investment; fantastic, now you have to create a return for your investors.

Your national board of directors accepted your business plan; Now you have to deliver the plan.

The company you pitched to love your ideas to transform their marketing; now you have to turn ideas into actions, and actions into results.

You had a great day showcasing your new premises; justifying them starts the day after.

It is great having big business days. Savour them. Photograph them. Enjoy them. Celebrate your achievement. And then deliver on them.

Here are a few tips on delivering on your big business day promises:

Start working on the delivery of what you promised /agreed the very next day. Don't risk waiting and losing momentum.

If you haven't done so in advance, timescale the implementation plan. Be accountable for the timescale. It is so easy in business to let things slip.

You organise a meeting of colleagues to get the plan moving but then something new comes along and the meeting gets re-arranged. Then two of the team can't make the new meeting. In the blink of an eye, three weeks have passed and you've done nothing.

Make the plan visible. Online on an internal shared system or physically via diagrams and grids placed around your offices which everyone can see.

Brief all of your team on what happened, and talk them through the implementation plan and their roles within that. Internal communication is a hazard in many businesses. The pandemic and the resulting increase in working from home has added to the communication challenge.

Check in on progress on a daily basis.

Why do all this?

Some companies and individuals are great at ‘winning’ business.

They’re not so great at delivering.

The ‘completer/finisher’ bit.

With the ‘win’ in the bag, their focus switches to the next ‘win’ opportunity.

The biggest ‘at risk’ plans are internal ones.

Your colleagues are excited following your presentation, but then nothing happens.

They think it was all just ‘lip service’.

Treat internal plans at the same level of importance as client ones.

SECTION SUMMARY - TOP BUSINESS TIPS: YOUR BIG BUSINESS DAY

- Agree on the desired outcome you want to achieve
- Set aside plenty of time to prepare
- During preparation, keep checking in on the desired outcome
- Be ruthless about leaving out stuff that won't affect the outcome
- Keep all key parties in the loop
- If your big day involves a presentation or pitch, rehearse it
- And then rehearse it again
- Reflect on why you won / why you lost
- Irrespective of the outcome, ask yourself 'now the big day is over if we did it again what would we do differently?'
- Start the implementation immediately, so momentum isn't lost

10.
THE AFTERMATH

On Sunday May 23rd, the day after the Classic Quarter, I was genuinely surprised as to how good my legs felt in the morning, and I was able to jog a little bit as we headed down towards Maenporth beach. Must have been the sand-coloured bath salts!

In the sea, I spent 15-20 minutes up to the top of my thighs in the cold water, walking up-and-down, up-and-down, up-and-down. The sea is great for post run recovery. We then went out to brunch, and I found my appetite had returned.

Had I really done this?

A feeling of euphoria that 'yes I had', combined with a sense of 'it was over'. Mixed emotions for sure.

On Sunday evening I recorded a podcast with Andy Williams. Andy and I had run the Classic Quarter as a relay of two in 2020, and although he left it quite late to enter we both then did it solo in 2021.

During the recording, we shared our run day experiences, shared tips and advice to potential CQ runners, and generally enjoyed reflecting on our big day out. Andy had a storming run, racing round in ten and a half hours. I did point out that although I was a lot slower, I did finish on the 'podium' in my age category. That recording is currently the most downloaded episode of the Running 44@60 podcast.

I had also recorded snippets every three miles during the run. Those recordings were okay but the wind was just a little bit too much in places, meaning it wasn't great quality despite the 'best' fluffy thing I had bought to go over the microphone to prevent wind intervention.

I used my phone for the recordings, but unfortunately it ran out of battery after about 10 hours. I don't think that was helped by me trying, three miles in, to add one of my crew to my 'find friends' app, with very little signal on the cliff tops.

I didn't realise at the time that the app was from that moment on trying to connect. That must have been what drained the battery. It meant no recordings during the last three hours, including reaching the finish. In the grand scheme of things, a minor inconvenience. Pre-run, if I had had to pick something that wouldn't quite work out, I would take the phone battery draining over picking up an injury, falling over on the rocks or hitting the 'wall'.

'INTO THE SEA THE NEXT DAY - I WAS AMAZED HOW GOOD MY LEGS FELT'

I'm not the greatest or most patient podcast editor, so stitching together about ten snippets plus a top and tail took a while, but no doubt worth it since it created the landmark episode 60 of the Running 44@60 podcast.

Ensuring that the on the run episode was number 60 meant recording two or three others immediately prior to the run, with imaginative titles such as '36 hours to go' (episode 58) and 'thanks to all my supporters' (episode 59).

On the Monday I went for a sports massage with Lee Wheston . I was feeling kind of pleased with myself when Lee told me that he felt my legs were in actually better nick than they had been on the previous Thursday, before the run, when he'd been concerned about a couple of small knots in my hamstrings.

His diagnosis made me feel pretty elated! I was clearly a highly tuned athlete! Or maybe I just hadn't pushed hard enough...

I had kept the Monday and Tuesday clear in my work diary. I'm not a great fan of social media, but it was nice to see all the kind comments that appeared. I wanted to enjoy and acknowledge my 15 minutes in the limelight!

I answered all the comments individually. A few more donations came in, but interestingly, from the point about 48 hours after the run had finished, the donations literally dried up. The Children's Hospice fundraising team had suggested donations would continue and I might get another 10-15% post event. That didn't happen, but I was already past the target and more than happy with the amount raised.

Kit unpacking revealed just how much food I had taken! Food waste is a hot topic. I aimed to try and recycle all the stuff I hadn't eaten, although by then I really didn't fancy squashed hot cross buns coated in crunchy peanut butter or banana bread that no longer resembled banana bread!

I updated my website so the new message on the front page and on my email signature became: 'I completed the Classic Quarter on May 22nd'.

A business lesson here is making sure that the information that is in the public domain about you is up-to-date because if it isn't that potentially reflects on the perception of you.

The LinkedIn post I put up created by far and away the biggest reaction, with 30 to 40 comments. Usually I'm lucky if my LinkedIn posts attract more than five or six comments. Perhaps it's the 'human' element rather than the matter-of-fact business stuff that ultimately people prefer to see.

On the Tuesday the video came out from the photographers, Simon and Anna Burt, about three and a half minutes long, and featuring snippets from the run and my post finish 'interview'. A super souvenir for me and a great way for them to be involved. Thanks Simon and Anna!

I do think when you have achieved a big goal, or a Big, Hairy, Audacious Goal you need to celebrate it and remember it.

Later, I would frame the course map with all the segment posts it notes, pin the banners and boards my crew created to the walls in my 'gym', and frame a couple of finish line photos. I also had my finisher's medal engraved. No doubt sometime in the future someone will find it and hopefully be interested in what I did. Or maybe not!

My finisher's running shirt is in on my office, discreetly placed so that whenever I'm on a Zoom call it is visible. I love it when people ask 'what's that running shirt behind you?'. I'm quick to respond - 'Funny you should ask...'

On the Thursday I did my first proper exercise post run - I went for a cricket practice net, and then the following Saturday, a week after the event I did play cricket. I was knackered afterwards! I honestly felt more tired after the cricket than I had after the run, so I think it's clear that you need to rest before the run and rest after the run!

Inevitably, a week after the event there was a definite lull in interest, including from myself, so one of the things that I did start to do in the first week was to get cracking on pulling this book together, knowing if I waited too long it wouldn't happen.

My body was recovering, my sleep pattern returned, the buzz died down, the social media comments drifted to a halt.

If you are inspired to do something like this, then be proud of yourself when you achieve it. Enjoy the moment and the immediate aftermath.

But be prepared for the time when the aftermath becomes a lull. It is over. Job done.

The question you will be asked is 'what next?' Don't leave it too long between completing your challenge or goal and setting the next one.

I set a deadline of June 10th, which would have been my mother's birthday, to conclude the fundraising campaign and effectively close out 44@60.

On reflection, reaching the £100/mile target had felt like a massive achievement in itself, particularly after that first masterclass which attracted two people!

Eventually reaching £6,600, or £150 a mile, was amazing and everyone who made that happen is listed in the appendix.

FOLLOWING UP

I guess the business equivalent of the aftermath is following up.

When your big business day is over clearly there is a sense of relief, particularly if it went well.

The next goal is to keep the momentum going that your big day created, avoiding feeling as though everything has gone flat after the big day build up, and ensuring you don't lose sight of what you did on the big business day.

That usually means following up. And in business we're not always great at following up.

Start the follow up process immediately, ideally the same day. You'll be feeling good, you'll be energised so don't even wait until tomorrow. Sleeping can lose you momentum!

So how to follow up?

Check on your goals for the big day. Did you achieve some or all of them?

Ideally you will have prepared your follow-up plan in advance. This is particularly important if your big day is full-on all day, such as exhibiting at a major event. It's easy to wait until you're 'back in the office' before you make contact with everyone who visited your stand and expressed interest in your offering. Those same people will have interacted with other exhibitors. The 'first to market' principle really does work for exhibitors. If you're the first company to contact me post-event, you clearly have a better chance of gaining my attention than if you are the tenth or twentieth person to contact me. And make your contact a good one.

A personalised message on LinkedIn, a phone call, a text, or a video email are all so much better than a standard text-based email. Especially if that email isn't personalised and just feels like it's a mass one that has been sent to all attendees.

The same principle of following up applies if your big day was a sales pitch, an event or client presentation, an internal briefing, or a meeting with investors.

'DON'T RISK LOSING MOMENTUM BY NOT FOLLOWING UP STRAIGHT AWAY'

You can do a cracking job on the day but that will be wasted if you don't have a robust pre-planned follow up process.

Start following up as soon as you have finished your big day delivery!

With the run, I found that people were interested and talking about it for a few days afterwards, but by the time a week had gone by, interest had clearly waned, the fundraising had dried up and everyone had moved on.

And that is what happens in business. The momentum and interest you create with your big pitch, or presentation, or presence at an event, or new product launch, or move to new premises, or the start of your new important role, won't last very long in the eyes of the masses.

There is a saying in business that 'the waters close over very quickly', and what we mean by that is that you can be the star player, the big chief, the great innovator, the main attraction, the best presenter etc... in your company or your sector, but then as soon as you move on or time passes, someone will take your place. And no matter how heartfelt the messages were when you announced you were moving on, as soon as the new kid on the block arrives, you become a distant memory very quickly.

My dad was, in his day, the captain of his golf club. The captain's journey started by becoming vice captain for the preceding year, and then captain for a year. As with others before him he was advised that 'there is nothing as past as a past captain', and the day you hand over to the person who was your vice captain is the day everything suddenly stops, with the exception I think at the time that the past captain enjoyed a designated parking spot for the year that followed captaincy!

The point here is that you need to enjoy the accolades of your big business day, but make the big business day the start of the journey to a bigger long-term goal.

Don't dwell on your success on the day for too long before you start to plan whatever it is you need to do next along your journey, and that's what a lot of people said to me after the run: 'so what's next Trevor?'

And what I said was that I'm going to write a book about my adventures and link it to business lessons, the very book that you are now reading!

Don't wait too long therefore to follow up your business idea or proposal or pitch, because your audience may well also witnesses similar pitches, proposals etc... and what you don't want is the waters to close over yours too quickly, which could well happen if you don't follow up.

Similarly, as I mentioned in the run aftermath section, if your big business day creates social media interest, then do respond to any comment that people make on your posts or if you've been tagged into something. And do it quickly. That will help you recognise that this is a great opportunity if you wish to start a conversation with somebody which doesn't have to continue on the public platform but can be moved over into a message situation, or phone call or a Zoom call or a visit or whatever.

Following up is one of the business situations I get asked about more than most. People say to me that prospective customers show lots of interest in the product or service but then when they attempt to recontact with them, they find it very difficult to get hold of them and restart the conversation.

Likewise they also say that if they get to the stage of putting forward a pitch or proposal, they become convinced at the time that the prospects are really interested, and then are always slightly disillusioned and disappointed when they send out a follow-up written proposal and hear absolutely nothing ever again.

One of my tips here is to be quite robust in that first meeting, particularly when people are signalling that they are genuinely really interested in what you are offering. My tactic is to utilise what I call 'mini commitments', in other words, confirming and clarifying every time someone says yes or nods their head or suggests that that is what they are looking for.

Something along the lines of: 'Just so I've understood what you are saying, am I right in thinking that you think this product or service would be able to........ for you?'

I would do that several times in the initial conversation or pitch. If you think the prospect is showing false signs of interest, which a lot of people do mainly because our default position in-person is to be encouraging rather than disparaging, then one of the tactics that I work with my clients on is to be quite robust in almost pushing the prospect towards telling you, 'No I'm not interested.'

My preferred tactic on this score would be, at the end of the conversation, to round up all the mini commitments and see how many I have, and if it's not that many then I give the client/prospect a chance to say no there and then.

It might be that you say something along the lines of 'It would be better if you tell me now if you're not interested, because that will save me time putting together further proposals, and save you time avoiding taking my follow-up calls and answering my follow-up messages.'

Some people might say this is a risky tactic because you are inviting the prospect to walk away from your idea, but let's face it, a lot of ideas are rejected, and in a lot of cases we are never told why they've been rejected, as prospects simply ignore our calls and email messages.

Bear in mind that, psychologically, this tactic takes away the prospect's power, to a degree. You are suggesting that they say no, and as a potential buyer we like to feel as though it should be our decision to make, not the seller's.

Sometimes that can have a surprisingly positive effect.

Whatever your business big day involved, then if you do the follow-up correctly it should inevitably create some opportunities for you.

Enjoy your big business day, but make sure you don't waste it by not following up.

SECTION SUMMARY - TOP BUSINESS TIPS: FOLLOWING UP

- Prepare your follow-up plan in advance

- Implement it straight away - ideally the same day

- Make the follow-up personal

- During the follow-up, focus on the benefits prospects will enjoy from your offering

- If your big day generates social media comments etc... reply to them all individually and quickly. They can be the start of 'offline' conversations that ideally are the first step to a business relationship

- If you are following up a business proposal you sent out, don't send an email asking, 'did you get my proposal?' or 'have you read my proposal?' or 'what did you think to my proposal?'

- Instead follow up with some added value - a link to a relevant article, an additional idea, even another alternative

- Include alternatives in all follow ups - alternative dates / times for a next meeting, three variations of your core proposal, etc

- Buyers like to make decisions. If you only offer one date /time or one buying option for your product or service then it becomes 'take it or leave it'

11.
IF I CAN DO IT

Lots of people commented on how they thought the 44@60 challenge was awesome but that there was no way that they could do something like that themselves.

I disagree.

When I announced in February 2019 I was going to tackle the Classic Quarter, running a half marathon was a challenge. Which is why my original goal had been to run a third career marathon when I was 60. That would be 11 and 16 years after my first two. At the time, thinking about running a third marathon was daunting enough.

I had joined Truro Running Club in October 2018. My son had just started medical school in Brighton. My daughter was at the Royal Welsh School of Music in Cardiff. I had no day-to-day responsibilities!

I admit that I joined the running club thinking it would be good for meeting new people. I imagined there would be lots of socialising around some running. Perfect. It would get me out of the house on a Wednesday night for a run. I'm not really an evening run person so I knew left to my own devices it was highly unlikely I'd be out pounding the streets of Truro on a wet Wednesday evening.

At the point of joining the running club I was parkrunning, having discovered that in early 2017. I imagine readers of this book will be fully aware of parkrun. If you're not check it out.

It's such a great thing to take part in as either a runner or a volunteer.

I was doing other bits of running and occasionally entering races. My running diary shows that in 2017 I did a total of 33 runs. That was about average for me. I had done 113 runs in 2005 when training for the Amsterdam marathon and 100 in 2010 when I ran the Eden marathon.

'YOU CAN RUN AN ULTRAMARATHON - YOU JUST NEED TO GO FOR IT'

Between 2011 and 2017 the most runs I did in a year was 51 and the least 24. Of those 33 in 2017, almost all were parkruns. I wasn't on Strava and beyond notes in my running diary I didn't record distances. The diary suggests my longest run in 2017 was just under six miles in 64 minutes. Not sure what I would have said at that stage if someone had suggested at the end of 2017 that in three and half years' time I'd be running 44 miles.

At the point of joining the running club in mid October 2018 I was up to 43 runs for the year, with the only organised one being the local Mawnan Smith 10k. My diary says 'first 10k for years'. My time was 58:40. The village event was very much a local run but had loads of lavish prizes. I remember that had I run the 5k event in half my 10k time I would have won my age category and a meal for two at a local pub!

Going to that first Truro Running Club club night was a game changer. I have no doubt that I would not have contemplated or certainly completed the Classic Quarter without being a member of the running club. As with parkrun, if you're reading this and you're not a member of your local running club, go and give them a try. Running clubs inadvertently often have a perception barrier in the eyes of potential new members. It's easy to assume that you have to be fit and fast to join a running club. Not so. Most, like ours in Truro, accommodate run/walkers right through to ultra runners and everyone in between.

There was a touch of *déjà vu* though on that first night. Back in 2012 I found myself on business for two nights in Cheltenham. I looked up the local running club, made contact and asked if I could come along. They were very welcoming. They did a run where you set off in one direction until you heard a whistle and then you came back. I must have over egged my ability as it was soon clear I was in the wrong group as they sped off into the distance!

Roll forward to my first club night in Truro and the same thing happened.

The designated activity that evening was called 'out and back'. I didn't know what that was, but listening to the organiser I gathered that some people were going to run 15 minutes, others 20 minutes and others 25 minutes.

I wrongly assumed that meant those were the times they were going to run the out and back challenge in. One group would take 15 minutes to do the route right through to the final group taking 25 minutes. That was the group for me. The slowest one.

Except that wasn't how it worked. There was no set distance. The 15 minute group would run as far as they could in 15 minutes, have a one minute rest and see if they could run back in less than 15 minutes. The same for 20 and 25. We did a steady ten minutes warm up to the local Dunelm. And then it was go. Not just go for my group but gone! They all raced off. I felt like one of those racehorses who gets tailed off early on in a race and pulls up. I was soon tailed off but 'pulling up' was not an option.

To the rescue came Colin Bathe. Each run had two 'leaders'. One at the front setting the pace, one at the back cajoling the stragglers. Or on this occasion the singular straggler. Me.

Colin was the club chairperson. He kept me company and chatted to me all the way round. It was mainly him chatting because I was doing a lot of sucking in air. This was the hardest run I'd had for some time. And the longest. Little did either of us know that in autumn 2021 I would succeed Colin as club chair. Had he not marshalled me around that run I might not have returned the following week.

When the run was finally over I was tired but elated. My 1920s Garmin showed I had run seven miles. Seven miles! And in 70 minutes! My longest run since the Woolacombe Bay half marathon in June 2016.

In sport you often hear the term 'marginal gain' - the small adjustments that make you slightly faster or stronger or higher. Parkrun is a great way of measuring progress.

My marginal gains were always highly motivating. Having survived that first club night, I was keen for more.

If you're reading this book and you're thinking, 'that must have been great, but I could never do it', then my question would be - 'why not?'

We are all potentially capable of great things. We just need convincing.

It was Jim Lawless who convinced me.

Once you're convinced, don't let the moment escape. What could be seen as bravado can quickly be overwhelmed with 'reality'. Too much reality. Too much doubt. Too much overthinking.

'This is crazy. There's no way I could do that.'

Once you've set your running BHAG in motion, you'll have to overcome plenty of times when you start seeking ways of dropping the idea.

Don't let that happen. Be determined. Be focused. You can do it. Think about how you will feel when you've achieved it.

I'm re-writing this section on a Friday in October 2021. On Wednesday at club night, a lady in my group had run the London Marathon three weeks earlier. She won't mind me saying that she hadn't regarded herself as a runner, and she was, how should I say, coming to running later in life. 18 months before London she started 'couch to 5k'.

At club night she was still on a high. Still not quite believing she had run the London Marathon.

And there's the reason for going for it and then going through with it. Your achievement will be something to be hugely proud of. Something you can look back on and say, 'I did that'.

So if I can do it - so can you.

Do it now.

Stop reading this book and set yourself BHAG!

And you're never too old!

I was 60.

In the all the years prior to my 60th birthday I had run two marathons - when I was 44 and 49.

Within seven months of that landmark birthday I had doubled my marathon count and run an ultra.

Christopher McDougall, in his book Born to Run: A Hidden Tribe, Superathletes, and the Greatest Race the World Has Never Seen said:

'You don't stop running because you get old, you get old because you stop running'

When we are faced with a Big, Hairy, Audacious Goal in business, sometimes it's not our colleagues or our customers or even our competitors that we have to convince that we are capable of delivering on the goal. It ourselves we need to convince.

It is easy for me to sit here and write about the need to have confidence in your own ability, about thinking positively all the time, about seeing the goal and going for it.

All of us will have some self-doubt, which in turn will create opportunities for us to talk ourselves out of delivering, or even trying to deliver, the big goal that we have set ourselves.

Professor Steve Peters wrote a famous business book called 'The Chimp Paradox', which deals with this very thing – on one shoulder you've got your positive attitude and on the other shoulder your negative one.

The question is, which one will win?

It is very easy to allow the negative one to win. With the run, in the two years building up to it, I'm sure if I analyse the situation I could point to loads of reasons or things that were happening that I could have turned into a 'well it was a good idea at the time but I've given up on it – it's never going to happen.'

When I reflect on that, I realise just how important a combination of the podcast and the fundraising were, at their own particular times.

Launching the podcast, around 22 months before when I thought the run was going to take place, was in hindsight excellent timing. I never committed to publishing episodes with a weekly frequency, unlike my business podcast. But what did happen was every time I did record an episode, either in an interview format or with me sharing what I was up to, it reinforced in my own mind that this was for real and that I was definitely going to do this.

'DON'T BE PUT OFF BY THOSE WHO TELL YOU IT WON'T / CAN'T WORK'

In the section called 'Shouting' I talked about how every time I met somebody I tried to weave the 44@60 into the conversation. Doing that it made it feel real.

So my message is that if you have set yourself a business goal and doubts are now creeping in, then talk about it to your colleagues, your customers, your peers, a business coach, and your family, and talk to them about it in a very positive, 'this is going to happen' tone.

I'm sure you will all have read about surrounding yourself with positive people. That doesn't mean the ones who tell you that everything you do or every idea you have is 'brilliant'.

Very often those are the people who actually have no real interest in your idea, they just think if they use the word 'brilliant' it will be motivational for you – which may well be the case. What you really want are people who are positive with a dose of realism.

Then there are the negative mindsetters. Most people are often in this camp. They are the ones whose natural inclination is to focus on why something won't work, rather why it will work. Usually they're not deliberately setting out to be negative, it just happens. I think it's linked to change. Most people resist change. They become experts at knowing something they've never used or tried before won't work for them.

You see this in business all the time. Think about the massive change that happened in early 2020 when the pandemic struck. People stopped going to their offices. They stopped visiting clients and prospective clients. Their company cars sat idle outside their houses.

'But don't worry, we've got Zoom', was the message. 'You can talk to your client face to face, share ideas on screen, make calls outside of 'normal' times if that suits them better.'

And then the response: 'You can't build business relationships on Zoom. And anyway we'll soon be back to spending hours travelling to a meeting the client has forgotten is happening, or can now only give us 15 minutes and not the 40 we were expecting.'

Sound familiar?

I'm sure all of you reading this book will know family, friends or colleagues who will focus on either saying your idea is 'brilliant', or giving you ten reasons why it won't work.

For the latter group in particular, you have to tolerate their negativity. Bear in mind that often these people don't realise they are being negative - it's just the way they come across. Even their tone of voice can bring you down!

Don't let them become the Harry Potter dementors - sucking the energy and life out of your idea or goal!

Focus on those who believe it is possible, even if it does sound somewhat crazy.

And be wary of talking yourself out of it as well. There will be plenty of times when you'll need to be saying to yourself 'come on you can do this.'

When I work with sales teams or companies seeking revenue growth, I share with them my 'CROPS Circle'. A simple diagram which shares the 5 steps to sales success. Conversation > Relationship > Opportunity > Pitch > Sale. There is an outer circle to this model with three things which will help you successfully deliver the CROPS steps:

Knowledge, Attitude and Mindset.

Knowledge is simply knowing everything about your client, your offering, your marketplace etc...

Attitude is the way you interact with people - customers, potential customers, colleagues...

Mindset is believing in yourself - that you can achieve your goals, do something different, be successful....

Ultimately though there is only one person who is leading the charge in your destiny to achieve your goal, and that is you.

You will be bored of me now talking about preparation and planning, so I promise this is the last time, but I make no excuses for labouring the point.

Having that roadmap to success is important. You need to know where you are aiming to go (your BHAG) and the route to follow to get there.

Be ready to be flexible though. The route doesn't always go exactly as you planned it. From time to time you will have to pivot and do things differently.

And sometimes that will simply be because you have found a better way of doing things.

My plan for the run pivoted several times, not drastically, but just sufficiently to help make it successful, and usually those pivots were driven when a piece of advice or a good idea emerged such as back-to-back training runs in the last three to four months, something I had not considered or even been aware of.

Eating watermelon and drinking flat Coke, briefing my crew in advance to tell me I was looking great even if I wasn't, eating six times a day in the last three or four weeks, ensuring that during the taper time, even on the shortest runs I ran at ultra-pace.

As I emphasised in the learning section, to be successful you have to keep learning, but that doesn't mean taking on board and doing everything that anybody suggests. It means giving everything due consideration, not ruling anything out, but ultimately being decisive about what you think will work best for you as you seek to attain your goal.

And then getting out there and making it happen!

SECTION SUMMARY - TOP BUSINESS TIPS: YOU CAN DO IT

- Set a Big, Hairy, Audacious Goal
- Share it and talk about it, a lot
- The more you talk about it the more real it will feel
- Watch out for dementors, those who (inadvertently) pick out why it won't work
- Be similarly wary of those who say its 'brilliant'
- Find people in between. Those who will encourage and advise but stay real
- Be prepared to pivot on your journey
- Keep track of all the parts of the goal - confidence in the overall goal being achieved will grow as parts of it are achieved
- Be ready for the times when you have doubts, when it would be easy to find excuses not to carry on - don't talk yourself to of it!
- Visualise what it will be like when you achieve your goal, and use that image as your motivation

WHAT NEXT?

RUNNING

I've got a new BHAG!
January 27th 2024
Arc of Attrition 50

This event starts at 8:30am at the Minack Theatre - the site of the last check point in the Classic Quarter. It then goes to Land's End and follows the North Coast via St Ives to Porthtowan. I crewed for the aforementioned Andy Williams in 2022. Why 2024 and not 2023? Like with the Classic Quarter I need about two years to plan it. That will include running the route in stages during the summer of 2022 and then in the winter of 22-23 running the sections at night on own which will be in the dark during the run. For me that will be most of the route from St Ives to the finish.

BUSINESS

I'm going to write a second book in 2022.
Working title 'How to deliver confident and successful presentations'

Via my 'Better Presentations More Sales' podcast, my 7P's of presenting model, blog articles and presentation skill programmes I've created and run I have tons of content waiting to be turned into a book!

I'm excited about both challenges!

12.
TOP TIPS FOR FIRST TIME ULTRA RUNNERS

I'm going to finish the book with a summary of my top tips for first time ultra runners and then my top 7 tips for business success which can be used by businesses of any size and at any stage of development. Running ones first:

- Pick a time of year, pick an ultra, fill in the entry form!

- Study the route - recce bits if you can - get a feel for it - visualise running it

- Divide the route into sections that you can easily manage - for me that was three mile sections

- Organise a crew - their support on the route will be invaluable

- Tell everyone what you're doing - it makes it feel real and I found the more I talked about it the more my confidence grew

- Keep a training diary - in a notebook but also on a public platform - a blog say - and on Strava - again encouraging comments from friends / other runners will give you a boost

- Stock up on carbs in the last couple of days

- Have a big porridge breakfast

- Start eating early during the run

- Take gels steadily throughout

- Keep sipping drinks all the time

- Have a salt tablet every hour

- Flat Coke is good in the second half

- Watermelon and baby tomatoes give you both energy and hydration

- Walk the hills in the event but run them in training

- Use running poles to help you up all the hills and steps. If that means spending a minute or two opening them up and putting them back it's worth it

- As the ultra nears its conclusion, keep shuffling along on the flats and downhills. Walking for too long may make it really hard to start running again

- Running the last part with someone else will help keep you going

- Look forward to the big day!

- Enjoy the big day!

- When it's over come on the Running 44@60 podcast and tell me all about it. Get in touch via podcast@trevorleemedia.co.uk

13.
7 TOP BUSINESS TIPS

1. Make it easy for your customers to understand what you are offering, to understand why they need it, the benefits it will bring them and how to buy it.

2. When they do look to buy your offering, make it as easy as possible for them, and check to see if there are any barriers to sales in place. These are often hidden, and particularly hidden to you and your colleagues. They are often only spotted by customers who are keen to buy but then don't.

3. Whenever you have any sort of customer interaction, whether that be a phone call, a meeting, presentation, pitch etc. have a clear purpose as to what you want the outcome of that interaction to be.

4. Be proactive and make things happen – if you are focused on being reactive, i.e. waiting for things to happen before you take action, you may well be successful for a period of time but eventually that will catch up with you.

5. Be a good listener and a good asker of questions. Asking questions will generate opportunities, providing that you ask really good questions and you listen carefully to the answers.

6. Believe in yourself, your business, your offering.

7. Be lucky!

14.
THE LIST OF THANKS

When you undertake something like this you realise just how important it is to have lots of people around you providing support and encouragement.

I am so grateful to so many people for helping make this happen. Whatever you are listed for below was hugely appreciated.

I hope I haven't missed anyone - apologies if I have.

So a big thanks to:

The Magnificent Crew:

Bethany - head of crew team
Craig - head of enthusiasm
Jim & Cass - sign makers and lollipop suppliers
Annabel & Nigel - last stop suppliers, transport to and from the start and finish

The Video and Photographers:

Simon and Anna Burt

The Event Organisers:

Endurancelife - James, Jordan, Flinn and the gang who ensured I was wearing number 60 during 44@60 and provided constant encouragement at all the check points.

The Runners:

Sam Pickering - providing valuable company and tour guide services over the last 15 miles
Andy Williams - for being the other half of the relay of two during the practice run in 2020

The Podcast Guests sharing top ultra running tips:

Edward Chapman
Colin & Nik Bathe
Andy Goundry
Mark Picken
Anna Pascoe
Francis Clark Ultra Team
Davie Hall
Loyd Purvis
Stuart and Rachel Thomson
Phil Begnett

Specialist Advisors and Helpers:

Loyd Purvis - shoes and gear
Lee Wheston - sports massage
Lou from the Run Lab - running style, gait and cadence
Anna Pascoe - Plan for the taper
Daz Stephens - Nutrition

The Charity:

The team at Children's Hospice South West who made me feel very special as a fundraiser for them.

The Birthday Marathon Support Runners:

Adrian Tyas
Tom Moore
Claire Mensing
Andy Williams
Laura Pool
Mark Thomas
Imogen Parnham-Kenny

Mark Trebilcock
Liz Trebilcock
Ralph Graves
Claire Palmer
Andy Stallard
James Skeplorn
Helen Mitchell
Bethany Lee

Businesses and Individuals that either attended the fundraising business Masterclasses, or hired me to deliver one of the masterclasses for their organisation:

St Austell Brewery
Bishop Fleming
Coodes
Miller Commercial
Make Me A Plan
Global Reach
Gripsure
AMS Instrumentation and Control
Space Professionals
Trailrunningman
Stacey Halfyard
Greg Hobbs
Joss Price
Chris Pawley
Imogen Parnham-Kenny
Elizabeth Stansfield
James Ferguson
Jane Barlow
Daz Stephens
Ric Reilly
Althea Stevens
Lisa Pascoe
Jane Potter
David Bone

Individual Sponsors:

Edward Chapman
Ali Loadman
Nick & Lucy Purkiss
Peter Watson
Grant Timms
Annabel Timmins
Amanda Berry
Eddie Dark
James & Jordache
Phil Jones
Jim Lawless
Mark Cant
Paul Higgins
Sue Lea
Ian Bishop
Andy Cooper
Tony Hazell
Adam Pearson
Jon Nance
Richard Greaves
Laura Walker
Rachel & Stuart Thomson
Keith Thompson
Andy Williams
Richard Alleger
John & Jill Mitchell
Linda Derry
Andrew Jones
Chris Dennis
Craig Lutton
Pete Ryan
Ric & Jo Lee
Celia & Matt Timms
Ian Piddington
Claire Mensing
Diccon Gray

Will & Lisa Lea
Harriet & Aaron
Ralph Graves
Bill & Val Reynolds
Paul & Maundrell
Mike Shaw
Christine Anthony
Amanda Eva
Alison North
Oli and Laura Pool
Stuart Pedlar
Mark Southcott
Nigel Hambly
Brian Dunstan
Paul & Lorraine Clements
Jim McKenna
Max White
Nikki Baron
Carl Bicknell
Jill & Henry Pooley
Martin Bravery
Inge Dowden
Martin Davies
Claire Palmer
Anton & Jane Luiten
Juliet Stewart
Colin & Nik Bathe
Jonty Wheatley
Suzie & Martin Hearn
Paul & Tricia Pearson
Nigel & Dawn Bishop
Nigel Knuckey
Becky & Kieran Head
Thomas Hewitt
Lorraine & Andy Brown
Jeremy Boase
Caroline Fardell

Tamsin Heayn
Shaun Hammond
Rebecca Morton
Phil Wheatley
Mustafa Shaikh
Sally Miller
Mary Stirling
Ann Robertson
Stuart Nye
Mick Mullen
Richard Vanhinsbergh
Charlie Wilkins
Simon Johnson
Carl Jolly
Davie Hall
Mandy Case
Rob Thompson
Tom Larkin
Ewan McClymont
Natasha Hennings
Garry & Lisa Tremayne
Barry & Marilyn
Sally Read
Gregory, Sylvia, Rachel Lutton
Katie Puremont
Sea to Summit
Kevin Hicks
Aaron Nihat
Malcolm & Marilyn
Tim & Jane Ballett

What a list!

If I have inadvertently missed you off the list, my apologies. There were a few people who donated anonymously, so thank you if that was you.

15.
CREW POINTS, FOOD, BOOKS, KIT

Here are the details of the crew points and the their what3words locations:

Praa Sands: thrusters.birthdays.canine

Marazion Cemetery: artist.relishing.complies

Raginnis Hill: absorbing.compacts.cable

Minack: soda.serenade.hoped

Ultra Running Books I read:

Running your first Ultra by Krissy Moehl
Running with the Kenyans by Adharanand Finn
Born to Run by Christopher McDougall
Fat Man to Green Man by Ira Rainey
The Rise of the Ultra Runners by Adharanand Finn
Achieve the Impossible by Prof Greg Whyte
Running up that Hill by Vassos Alexander
Running for their lives by Mark Whitaker
Above the Clouds by Kilian Jornet

Foods and Recipes:

Pre-Run Porridge:

Small cup of jumbo porridge oats
Small cup of coconut milk
Small cup of water

Mix well and cook on low heat for around 20 minutes
Pour on honey or maple syrup
Add a cut up banana

Flapjack recipe:

200 grams of porridge oats
100 grams of vegan margarine
75 grams of a combination of coconut and light brown sugar
Golden syrup not really measured but quite a bit

Melt very slowly the golden syrup with the margarine in a pan over low heat

And whilst that is going on prepare the dry ingredients to add to the porridge oats and sugars:

Chopped dates
Sultanas
Chia seeds
Flaxseed
Maca powder
Crunchy peanut butter

Mix all the dry ingredients. Stir in the melted syrup and margarine. Transfer to a baking tray and bake for 25 to 30 minutes at a temperature of about 140°C.

Leave for 5 minutes. Then cut into small blocks and transfer to a cooling rack.

Kit worn / carried:

Hoka Torrent 2 trail shoes
Hoka Rincon road shoes
Wigwam socks
Skins calf compressions
Saxx underwear

Sports shorts with pockets for flannels and hankie (for keeping running glasses clean and dry)
Truro Running Club t-shirt
Buff cap
Running glasses
Running gloves

Ultimate Direction hydration vest
Salomon waterproof jacket and cap
Spare base layer
Waterproof trousers
Face mask
Running poles
Glasses cleaning spray
Suncream
Sudacrem
Hand sanitiser
Head torch
Emergency first aid kit inc foil blanket
Phone
Podcast recording lapel microphone
Credit card
£20 note
20 pence pieces (for some loos if needed)

Note that a number of the items listed above were mandatory for this event

Foods and drink carried in the hydration vest:

Water
Torq isotonic drink
Flapjack
Hot cross buns with peanut butter
Banana bread
Torq gels
Blok - jelly baby type stuff
Ginger sweet/jelly type small bits

Jelly babies
Nakd bars
Mini Cheddars
Salt and vinegar crisps
Mini malt loaf
Salt tablets

Crew Items:

Extras of most of the above plus:
Road shoes
Vaseline
Flat Coca Cola
Watermelon
Baby tomatoes
Filled water and isotonic bottles for swap overs
Spare socks
Green tea in flask
Stretch band in case needed

And lots of words of encouragement!

16.
THAT'S IT - JOB DONE!

Running 44, almost 45, miles was a Big, Hairy, Audacious Goal.

Raising £100 per mile, that became £150 per mile, was a Big, Hairy, Audacious Goal.

Writing this book felt similar.

All three are things I'd never done before, never attempted, never considered.

I hope you've enjoyed the story.

I hope maybe it has inspired you to think you could set yourself a running or business or both Big, Hairy, Audacious Goal.

Go on.

You know you want to.

We don't always regret the things in life we do.

More often we regret the things we thought about doing and then didn't.

Printed in Great Britain
by Amazon

78986481R00122